# A CRITICAL ANSWER

## TO

## James Price's

## King James Onlyism

# D. A. WAITE, Th.D., Ph.D.

**225 of Price's Statements
Analyzed Carefully for
Errors, Misrepresentations,
and Serious Falsehoods**

# Published by

# THE BIBLE FOR TODAY PRESS
900 Park Avenue
Collingswood, New Jersey 08108
U.S.A.

Church Phone: 856-854-4747
BFT Phone: 856-854-4452
Orders: 1-800-John 10:9
e-mail: BFT@BibleForToday.org
Website: www.BibleForToday.org
fax: 856-854-2464

**We Use and Defend
the King James Bible**

**April, 2009**
**BFT 3375 BK**

Copyright, 2009
All Rights Reserved

ISBN #1-56848-063-6

# 𝕬cknowledgments

I wish to acknowledge the assistance of the
following people:

- **Dianne W. Cosby**--our daughter, for listening carefully to these messages that were broadcast by radio and by the Internet around the world; for typing these messages accurately from the cassette tapes; and for putting them into computer format to be used as the basis for this book.

- **Yvonne Sanborn Waite**--my wife, for encouraging the publication of these radio messages; for reading the manuscript carefully; for suggesting various boxes; and for giving other helpful suggestions for the body of the book and for the cover.

- **Barbara Egan**--our **Bible For Today** secretary, for proofreading the manuscript; for suggesting various corrections; and for making valuable comments.

- **Julia Monaghan**–a faithful supporter of our **Bible For Today** ministry and an attender via the Internet of our **𝕭ible 𝕱or 𝕿oday 𝕭aptist 𝕮hurch** services, who read the manuscript and gave helpful comments for correction.

- **Daniel S. Waite**--the Assistant to the **Bible For Today** Director, who kept my computer working properly; helped with the printing, and made important suggestions.

- **Dr. H. D. Williams**--a friend in the **Bible For Today** and the Dean Burgon Society ministries. His expertise in "print on demand" (POD) technology has made it possible for us to print this book in this manner, thus saving us thousands of dollars.

# FOREWORD

● *A Critical Answer to King James Onlyism: A New Sect* is a response to the book, *King James Onlyism: A New Sect*, written by Dr. James D. Price in 2006. According to an announcement for his book it is stated that Dr. Price *"was Professor of Hebrew and Old Testament at Temple Baptist Seminary in Chattanooga, Tennessee, from 1972 to 2005, and Academic Dean from 2000 to 2005."*

● Price has joined the BJU position in two areas: (1) disbelief in the preservation of the original Hebrew, Aramaic, and Greek Words, and (2) a strong opposition to those who maintain this position, referring to them as *"**King James Only**"* people which is a synonym for followers of the heresies of Peter Ruckman.

● In this book, I have quoted and given **COMMENTS** on 225 of Price's **STATEMENTS**. Though I have seen a brief refutation of Price's book, I do not know of any other thorough treatment. For this reason, I believe it is important to counteract some of the many falsehoods in Price's book more extensively. I hope those on both sides of the Bible Version debate will read this book in order to examine the many inaccuracies, misunderstandings, and falsehoods contained in Price's book.

● The reader is encouraged to get three of my recent books answering the BJU arguments on Bible versions and Bible preservation: (1) *Fundamentalist Deception on Bible Preservation* (**BFT #3234** @ **$8.00 + $4.00 S&H**), (2) *Bob Jones University's Errors on Bible Preservation* (**BFT #3259** @ **$8.00 + $4.00 S&H**), and (3) *A Critical Answer to Michael Sproul's God's Word Preserved* (**BFT #3308** @ **$11.00 + $4.00 S&H**). May the Lord give you discernment in this current battle for our Bible.

Sincerely yours for God's Words,

Pastor D. A. Waite, Th.D., Ph.D.
Director of the **Bible For Today**, Incorporated, and
Pastor of the **Bible For Today Baptist Church**

# Table of Contents

# A CRITICAL ANSWER

## to

## James Price's
## King James Onlyism:
## A New Sect

# Introductory Considerations

This book is an attempt to bring a partial answer and reply to a number of errors, misrepresentations, and serious falsehoods in James D. Price's book entitled *King James Onlyism: A New Sect*. According to the back cover of his book, here is some of the background of Dr. Price:

*James D. Price was Professor of Hebrew and Old Testament at Temple Baptist Seminary in Chattanooga, Tennessee, from 1972 to 2005, and Academic Dean from 2000 to 2005. He has a B.S. degree in Electrical Engineering from Purdue University, with 25 years experience in that profession, serving as a senior research engineer for Franklin Institute Research Laboratories in Philadelphia before moving to Temple Baptist Seminary. He has a M.Div. From Northwest Baptist Theological Seminary in Tacoma, Washington (formerly Los Angeles Baptist Theological Seminary), and a Ph.D. in Hebrew and Biblical Literature from Dropsie College for Hebrew and Cognate*

*Languages in Philadelphia. . . . "*

Dr. James D. Price certainly has some very fine qualifications to enable him to write such a book as he has written. In the interest of fairness, let me give the readers some of my own qualifications that enable me to answer such a book written by such a qualified Christian gentleman:

*"The author of this book, Dr. D. A. Waite, received a B.A. (Bachelor of Arts) in classical Greek and Latin from the University of Michigan in 1948, a Th.M. (Master of Theology), with high honors, in New Testament Greek Literature and Exegesis from Dallas Theological Seminary in 1952, an M.A. (Master of Arts) in Speech from Southern Methodist University in 1953, a Th.D. (Doctor of Theology), with honors, in Bible Exposition from Dallas Theological Seminary in 1955, and a Ph.D. in Speech from Purdue University in 1961. He holds both New Jersey and Pennsylvania teacher certificates in Greek and Language Arts.*

*He has been a teacher in the areas of Greek, Hebrew, Bible, Speech, and English for over thirty-five years in ten schools, including one junior high, one senior high, three Bible institutes, two colleges, two universities, and one seminary. He served his country as a Navy Chaplain for five years on active duty; pastored two churches; was Chairman and Director of the Radio and Audio-Film Commission of the American Council of Christian Churches; since 1971, has been Founder, President, and Director of THE BIBLE FOR TODAY; since 1978, has been President of the DEAN BURGON SOCIETY; has produced over 700 other studies, books, cassettes, VCR's, DVD's, or CD's on various topics; and is heard on a thirty-minute weekly radio program IN DEFENSE OF TRADITIONAL BIBLE TEXTS, on radio, and streaming on the Internet at www.BibleForToday.org. 24/7/365. Dr. and Mrs. Waite have been married since 1948; they have four sons, one daughter, and, at present, eight grandchildren, and eight great-grandchildren. Since October 4, 1998, he has been the Pastor of The Bible For Today Baptist Church in Collingswood, New Jersey. The Church Phone is: 856-854-4747."*

I call this reply to Price's book, *A CRITICAL ANSWER to JAMES PRICE'S KING JAMES ONLYISM: A NEW SECT.* I have made comment on 225 of Price's statements in his book in an attempt to answer the many errors, misrepresentations, and serious falsehoods that he has written. I could have written much more, and I am sure that Price could have written much more, but what we have both written, we have written.

# 225 of His Statements and My Comments-- Statements ##1-50

## Price Wrote A Large Book

**STATEMENT #1.** (p. iii) This book has an Introduction, seventeen Chapters, and Appendices A through J.

**COMMENT #1**. This is indeed a large book. It has 16 Roman numeral pages and 658 Arabic pages making a total of 674 pages in all. No one can say that Price has not attempted to write at great length about his point of view, despite the many errors, misrepresentations, and serious falsehoods. Though there are many more things I could say, I have limited myself to only 225 comments about the statements found in this book.    We are starting with the Preface.

## King James Only–A Ruckman Term

**STATEMENT #2.** (p. xiii) Price wrote: "*The King James Only controversy has been raging for over three decades*. *I first heard of it in the early 1970s*."

**COMMENT #2.** At the bottom of this page he also uses the term, "*King James Only*." As Price uses it throughout this book, this is a slanderous term. It is name-calling. I do not believe that I fit the description as it is used in this book.. **A "*King James Only*" person is like Peter Ruckman** and his followers. Ruckman, and those who follow him, believe that all that a person should have is the King James Bible, no matter what the mother tongue is. He doesn't believe you should have a Spanish or a French translation or any other translation. He doesn't believe you should use the Hebrew, Aramaic, or Greek, but the **King James Only**.

If Price were to confine this term to the Ruckmanites, that would be all right. But he does not do this. He uses the term to smear and blacken the reputations of those of us who stand for and defend the King James Bible and the Hebrew, Aramaic, and Greek Words that underlie it. I and others like me do not agree with the Ruckmanites that the English can correct the original Hebrew, Aramaic, and Greek Words that underlie it. I don't agree with that at all. Price has refused to clearly define and delineate his "**King James Only**" term and because of this has used it as a term of slander to those who are not followers of Peter Ruckman.

If Price is talking about the Ruckman position only, it may be "**over three decades**" old. But, if he is talking about my own position, Dean Burgon's position, and the position of the Dean Burgon Society and the **Bible For Today**, this is neither a "*sect*," nor a "*new sect*" as Price's book title claims. The people standing for the Traditional Greek Text are not a "*new sect*." It has been the belief of the Apostolic times to the present.

> There are many of us who stand for the original and preserved Hebrew, Aramaic and Greek Words that underlie our King James Bible and for the King James Bible as the only accurate translation of these preserved Words. This belief is not a "*new sect*" or a "*sect*." By using this term in his title (*"King James Only"*) and throughout his book, Price is smearing and slandering all of us who stand where we ought to stand on the Bible, implying that we're all followers of the heretical position of Peter Ruckman. I protest strongly!

It should be pointed out that James Price is a Critical Text only sect man. He is a Westcott and Hort text only sect man. He is a Nestle/Aland text only sect man. He is a United Bible Societies text only sect man. Price's "*sect*" is not a "*new sect*," but a very "*old sect*." In fact, it is an "*old cult*." It was begun by the heretical Gnostics in Alexandria, Egypt. The Gnostics were the ones who changed the Textus Receptus in over 8,000 places to give Price his perverted Greek text. His Gnostic Greek text has at least 356 doctrinal passages which are perversions of the truth.

# Price Cut His Teeth on the KJB

**STATEMENT #3.** (page xiii) *"In my early days, it never entered my mind that __the King James Version needed revision in modern English__ because __I cut my teeth on that edition of the Bible memorizing it from early childhood__. . . . It was not until I began teaching in seminary that I discovered I was investing a worthwhile percentage of my time __teaching Elizabethan English in my classes instead of Bible__."*

**COMMENT #3.** He "*cut his teeth*" on the King James Bible, and now he is downing it. Price did not need to "*teach Elizabethan English*" in his classes. If our *Defined King James Bible* had been around when he was teaching, he could have encouraged his students to get copies of the *Defined King James Bible*. Whenever his students (or anyone else now) would have read the King James Bible and didn't understand an uncommon word, they would have been able to find that word defined accurately in the footnotes. The King James Bible does not need a "*revision in modern English*," it is the only accurate translation of the preserved original Hebrew, Aramaic, and Greek Words.

---

# "Fair, Thorough, Honest, Courteous"?

**STATEMENT #4.** (p. xiv) "*I have tried to be fair, thorough, honest, and courteous in the way the matters are treated*."

**COMMENT #4.** As I will be pointing out in this critique, Price is not "*fair*." He is not "*thorough*." He is not "*honest*." Certainly he is not "*courteous*" in the way he smashes me and others who reliably stand for the King James Bible and the Hebrew, Aramaic, and Greek Words that underlie it. What Price should do is simply to say that there is a battle over the Greek Words underlying the King James Bible, and those underlying most modern versions. Instead of this, Price has instituted a vilification of those of us who have a sound, clear, and honest position on the King James Bible (as mentioned above) by calling us repeatedly "King James Only" and putting us into the same camp as that of Peter Ruckman. This is certainly not "*fair, thorough, honest, and courteous*." In fact, it is unfair, slipshod, dishonest, discourteous and rude. It ill behooves a Christian man of God such as Price to engage in such tactics while at the same time claiming that he has not done so.

# Final Authority–Hebrew/Greek/English?

**STATEMENT #5.** ". . . *King James Onlyism. The new doctrine declares that the King James Version of the Bible is the providentially preserved Word of God, and is actually (or essentially) the only and final authority in all matters of faith and practice for the English speaking world today*."

**COMMENT #5.** This is a definition of Ruckmanism. It's a definition of what Peter Ruckman believes. Our sound position on the King James Bible is that "*the only and final authority in all matters of faith and practice*" is not any translation, but is found in the Words of the preserved original Words of Hebrew, Aramaic, and Greek. This sound position is not a *"new doctrine"* but has been in the church from Apostolic times.

> If Price wants to fight with Peter Ruckman, that is fair game. But to mix Ruckmanism in with our sound position thus misrepresenting us is a deceptive, divisive, and devilish distortion. Price is mixing the Ruckman position and our sound position.

# KJB–Formerly Used Most Often

**STATEMENT #6.** (p. 1) " *In my early years . . . the King James Version of the Bible was the version used most often by people in those* [independent Baptist] *churches for studying and memorizing, and by preachers in the pulpit.*"

**COMMENT #6.** This is my position. I have been using the King James Bible ever since I was saved in 1944. That doesn't make me a follower of the "*King James Onlyism*" and a follower of Peter Ruckman. My use of the King James Bible in English doesn't mean that I don't stand for the preserved original Hebrew, Aramaic, and Greek Words that underlie the King James Bible. This is my position.

**STATEMENT #7.** (p. 1) "*The idea that the King James Version was the only Bible one could use was unheard of.*"

**COMMENT #7.** Growing up, as Price was "*in the 1930s and 40s,*" (p. 1), other than the English Revised Version of 1881 and the American Standard Version of 1901, the King James Bible was about the only Bible around in those early days.

# Final Authority–Hebrew & Greek

**STATEMENT #8.** (p. 1) "*Everyone in conservative Christian circles understood that the King James Version is one of the many translations of the Hebrew and Greek texts of the Bible, and that the final authority for faith and doctrine always has been the original Hebrew words written by Moses and the prophets and the original Greek words written by the apostles.*"

**COMMENT #8.** That is correct! The Hebrew and Greek words of the Bible are my "*final authority for faith and doctrine.*" However, the King James Bible is not just "*one of the many translations of the Hebrew and Greek texts of the Bible.*" It is the **only accurately translated** English translation **of the proper Hebrew, Aramaic and Greek Words**. This is a great distinction.

> `There are two things to be made clear: (1) The Hebrew, Aramaic, and Greek Words that Price espouses are not the proper ones. (2) The so-called "*many translations*" of those improper words used inaccurate translation technique.

In his book, Price repeatedly libels those of us who take a different stance with him (1) on the Hebrew, Aramaic, and Greek Words and (2) on the proper translation techniques to be used with the term "*King James Only*." In so doing, he equates us with the heretical views of Peter Ruckman. What Price should have done in his book, if he wanted to be honest about it, was either (1) to write a book against the views of Peter Ruckman and his followers or (2) to write a book outlining his disagreement with us on his false critical Bible texts and his false dynamic equivalent methods of Bible translation.

# Critical-Text-Men Machen & Wilson

**STATEMENT #9.** (p. 2) "*My professors had studied under such great fundamental scholars as G. Gresham Machen and Robert Dick Wilson. My Greek professors taught directly from the Greek New Testament .*"

**COMMENT #9.** This explains why Price has accepted as true and faithful the Gnostic manuscripts of Vatican and Sinai. Though indeed "*Machen*" and "*Wilson*" were "*great fundamental scholars*," they never saw the light about the Gnostic perversions but rejected the Traditional Received Greek Words as corruptions rather than seeing their own critical Greek texts as the true corruptions. It is strange that such "*fundamental scholars*" followed the Gnostic Greek text originally propounded by the anti-fundamental and heretical scholars, Bishop Brooke Foss Westcott (1825-1903) and Professor Fenton John Anthony Hort (1828-1892). This perverted text is now available with few alterations as either the Nestle/Aland text or the United Bible Societies text. Price studied under teachers who espoused false Gnostic Greek texts and never changed his views. I studied under the same false Gnostic Greek text and after about 20 years, I found the truth and rejected those false texts.

# RV, ASV, & RSV Not "Acceptable"

**STATEMENT #10.** (p. 2) "*The rejection was of theological liberal bias of the RSV, not to textual issues or a sudden need to have a final authority in English. Pastors continued to refer to the Greek and Hebrew, the RV and the ASV and other acceptable modern versions .*"

**COMMENT #10.** Here Price smears those of us who oppose his love of the Gnostic Greek texts and the inaccurate versions based upon them as though we have a "*final authority in English*." Despite my use and defense of the King James Bible, my "*final authority*" cannot be "*English*" and must not be English, Spanish, French, Russian, Chinese, or any other translation. It must be the preserved original Hebrew, Aramaic, and Greek Words. I believe those Words are those underlying the King James Bible.

As far as saying that the "*RV and the ASV*" are "*acceptable modern versions*," I could not disagree more. The "*RV*" refers to the English Revised Version (ERV) of 1881, commonly referred to as the "*RV*." The "ASV" refers to the American Standard Version (**ASV**) of 1902. It was the USA version of the English Revised Version (ERV) of 1881. These versions are not acceptable to me. They are acceptable to Price for two reasons: (1) He believes in the false Gnostic Greek text of Westcott and Hort (also known as Nestle/Aland or United Bible Societies). I dispute these texts. These are the texts underlying both the "*RV and the ASV*." (2) He agrees with the dynamic equivalence translation technique that has been, of a greater or lesser degree, in both the "*RV and the ASV*." I dispute this translation technique.

**STATEMENT #11.** (pp. 2-3) "*Henry C. Thiessen quoted from the RV and the ASV. Augustus H. Strong, Emery H. Bancroft, William Evans and other conservative theologians did the same.*"

**COMMENT #11.** Just because "*Henry C. Thiessen quoted from the RV and the ASV*" and these other "*conservative theologians*" did so, does this make these versions correct? Not at all. They are all mistaken as to this matter of Bibliology as is Price and as I was from around 1952 to 1972. The Revised Standard Version (RV) of 1881 and the American Standard Version (ASV) are based on a New Testament Gnostic Greek text that differs with that of the King James Bible in at least 8,000 words [See *8,000 Differences Between the Critical Text and the Traditional Text* by Dr. Jack Moorman (**BFT #3084** for a gift of $20.00 + $5.00 S&H)]. These altered words include doctrinal errors in at least 356 doctrinal passages [See *Early MSS, Church Fathers, & the Authorized Version* by Dr. Jack Moorman (**BFT #3230** @ $20.00 + $5.00 S&H.)]

# KJV--Not Only Acceptable Version?

**STATEMENT #12.** (p. 3) Price mentioned that in the 1960's he was a member of a "*GARBC church in Haddon Heights, New Jersey*." In that church, he said: "*There was not the slightest hint that anyone thought that the King James Version was the only acceptable Bible to use.*"

COMMENT #12. What Price does not say about his *Haddon Heights* Baptist Church, where he was a member, is that in the 60's there was no other Bible preached from or used except the King James Bible. The same was true when Mrs. Waite and I were members in the same church in the 80's and 90's. For over 100 years, the King James Bible was preached in that church. When that church stopped using that Bible, we left the membership. With the record of using the King James Bible, I would imagine that, in practice at least, that church really did believe that the King James Bible was indeed *the only acceptable Bible to use*. So we would have to disagree with Price in this statement as well.

## Price's Ruckman Smear

STATEMENT #13. (p. 4) *"It was not until the early 1970's, after I began to teach, that I first heard of the King James Only idea. I could not believe that anyone would advocate such a teaching. The first mention of the new doctrine came from a student of Peter Ruckman, and then from his own writings."*

COMMENT #13. This term describes *"Peter Ruckman"* and only *"Peter Ruckman"* and his followers. Price should have used it only in that way rather than trying to smash those of us who disagree with this Ruckman position yet use and defend the King James Bible and its underlying Hebrew, Aramaic, and Greek Words. By its very definition, *"King James Only"* means *"only"* the King James, and nothing else. Ruckman does not believe the Bible should be in Spanish, English, Russian, French or any other language. *Peter Ruckman* believes that *"only"* the King James English is the Bible. He believes the heresy that it was given by direct revelation from God.

On a telecast program hosted by John Ankerberg, one of *Peter Ruckman's* associates, Samuel Gipp, was asked what would a Russian do if he wanted to read God's Word. Samuel Gipp responded that the Russian would have to learn English and read the King James Bible. That is an erroneous position. Price falsely implies that Edward Hills, Jasper James Ray and David Otis Fuller were proponents of this *Peter Ruckman* heresy. Price is to be strongly reproved for these untruths. He should be more careful with the truth rather than slander these men in this way to attempt to allege that Hills, Ray, and Fuller hold to the "King James Only" position of *Peter Ruckman*.

In order for Price to prove this falsehood, he would have to provide from the writings of these men (which he cannot do) the following two significant things: (1) Clear proof that these men do **not** hold the Hebrew, Aramaic, and

Greek Words to be the "*final authority for faith and doctrine*." (2) Clear proof that these men believe the King James Bible to be "*given by inspiration of God*" (2 Timothy 3:16) as a "*revelation*" rather than a mere "*translation*" and, as such, supersedes the original Hebrew, Aramaic, and Greek Words of the originals, and therefore can correct those original words. Failing of that, Price should apologize to these three men and all the rest of us who have been falsely smeared and libeled by Price as "*Ruckmanites*," but who are not.

# Which Greek and Hebrew Texts?

**STATEMENT #14.** (p. 5) "*However, a study of history reveals the roots of fundamentalism rests in the authority of the Greek and Hebrew texts of the Bible, not in an English translation.*"

**COMMENT #14.** I would agree that "*the authority of the Greek and Hebrew texts of the Bible*" is the foundation of "*fundamentalism*." But the point of my disagreement with Price is the location of the "*Greek and Hebrew texts*." Price holds to a mixed Hebrew text and the Gnostic critical Greek text either of Westcott and Hort, Nestle/Aland, or United Bible Societies. I and others like me hold to the Hebrew, Aramaic, and Greek Words that underlie the King James Bible.

**STATEMENT #15.** (p. 5) Price's heading reads: "*Original Languages Authoritative for Baptists.*"

**COMMENT #15.** My questions is which "*original languages*" were "*authoritative*"? For the Old Testament, it was the pure Traditional Masoretic Hebrew Words, not Price's mixed Old Testament text with words other than the Traditional Hebrew Words only. For the New Testament it was the Textus Receptus underlying the King James Bible, not Price's Gnostic Greek texts of Westcott and Hort, Nestle/Aland, or United Bible Societies.

# Dean Burgon's TR/KJB Defense

**STATEMENT #16.** (p. 12) Speaking of Dean John William Burgon (1813-1888), Price wrote: "*Burgon was not a defender of the Textus Receptus that underlies the KJV, but of the Byzantine Text which he referred to as the Traditional Text.*"

**COMMENT #16.** That is a falsehood that many have perpetuated in this New Testament textual debate. Dean Burgon strongly defended the Authorized Version (KJB) and the text that underlies it. It is true that he said there were a few changes here or there that might be made, but he also made it very clear that before any changes are made to the Authorized Version (KJB) English there should be a complete and thorough analysis of all the evidence to be found in the Greek manuscripts. To get straightened out on how Dean Burgon would totally disagree with the so-called "*Byzantine Text*" of the so-called "*Majority Text*," Price should get a copy of my small paperback book entitled *Burgon's Warning on Revision* **(BFT #804 @ $7.00 + $4.00 S&H)**. In that booklet, I have quoted from Dean Burgon's *Revision Revised* **(BFT #611 @ $25.00 + $5.00 S&H)**.

> Here are two quotes from Dean Burgon about the Textus Receptus. Notice that, despite the fact that he feels that  *it requires Revision in respect of many of its lesser details*, he exalts this text both as to its reliability and its age. Both these quotations come from Burgon's *Revision Revised*, page 269:
>
> > *XIII. The one great Fact, which especially troubles him and his joint Editor,--(as well it may)--is The Traditional Greek Text of the New Testament Scriptures. Call this Text Erasmian or Complutensian,--the Text of Stephens, or of Beza, or of the Elzevirs,--call it the 'Received,' or the Traditional Greek Text, or whatever other name you please;--the fact remains, that a Text has come down to us which is attested by a general consensus of ancient Copies, ancient Fathers, ancient Versions.*" (Dean John W. Burgon, *The Revision Revised*, p. 269).

From this quotation, you can see that Burgon included the "*Received*" Text as another name for the "*Traditional Greek Text.*" Price is in error when he falsely claimed that Dean Burgon talked about " *the Byzantine Text which he referred to as the Traditional Text.*" In all 549 pages of Burgon's *Revision Revised*, he never once used the term, "*Byzantine.*" Nor did Burgon use that term in the 384 pages of his *Traditional Text*. Nor did Burgon use that term in the 400 pages of his *Last Twelve Verses of Mark*. Nor did Burgon use that term in his 302 pages of his *Causes of Corruption*. Nor did Burgon use that term in his 624 pages of his *Inspiration and Interpretation*. In other words, in a total of Dean Burgon's 2,259 pages of his five major works on the New Testament Greek Text, he never once used the term "*Byzantine*" which is what Price used as the same as the "*Byzantine Text.*" I suggest that Price should get a copy of all five of these books which our Dean Burgon Society has reprinted and are available either from www.DeanBurgonSociety.org or from www.BibleForToday.org and study every word of Dean Burgon's major works and stop putting words in his mouth which he never used.

> On this same page, Burgon said the following in support of the "Textus Receptus "*as it stands*":
>
> > "*Our Readers cannot have yet forgotten his virtual admission*

> *that,--Beyond all question the <u>Textus Receptus</u> is the dominant Graeco-Syrian Text of A.D. 350 to A.D. 400.₂ Obtained from a variety of sources, this Text proves to be essentially the same in all. That <u>it requires Revision in respect of many of its lesser details</u>, is undeniable: but <u>it is at least as certain that it is an excellent Text as it stands, and that the use of it will never lead critical students of Scripture seriously astray</u>,--which is what no one will venture to predicate concerning any single Critical Edition of the N. T. which has been published since the days of Griesbach, by the disciples of Griesbach's school. (Revision Revised, p. 269)*

How did Dean Burgon say these "*lesser details*" should be verified? In my opinion, changing any of the "*details*" of the Textus Receptus should be done in Burgon's way. But to this date, nobody has ever done this Burgon's way. The English Revised Version and the Westcott and Hort translators did not do it Burgon's way. The "*<u>Majority Text</u>*" (called the "*<u>Byzantine Text</u>*" by Price) of Hodges and Farstad (or of Robinson and Pierpont) did not do it Burgon's way.

To see exactly how Dean Burgon would verify any "*<u>details</u>*" about the Textus Receptus, I searched his *Revision Revised* for his methods. I summed them up in my booklet, *Burgon's Warnings on Revision* (BFT #804 @ $7.00 + $4.00 S&H). First, he said that the Textus Receptus "*is an excellent Text as it stands*" (*Revision Revised*, p. 269).

> On page 36 of BFT #804, here are some of Dean Burgon's prerequisites for revision of any "*<u>details</u>*" of the Greek text:
>
> √     1. "We need at least 500 more copies of the New Testament diligently collated." The Majority text has not done this. The Westcott and Hort Text did not do this.
>
> √     2. "We need at least 100 ancient lectionaries very exactly collated." This has never been done either.
>
> √     3. "We need the most important ancient versions to be edited afresh, and let their languages be really mastered by Englishmen." Have they done that? Of course they haven't. These are prerequisites for Dean Burgon to change any scintilla of the Textus Receptus that was standing in his day and is standing in our day.
>
> √     4. "We need above all the Church Fathers to yield their very precious secrets by ransacking them, indexing them, and diligently inspecting them." These four things are to be done before any changes are

done to the Textus Receptus. Until these things are done we must leave the Textus Receptus alone. Don't go along with Price's Westcott and Hort Text Onlyism. Don't go along with Price's Nestle/Aland Text Onlyism. Don't go along with Price's United Bible Societies Text Onlyism. This is stupidity. This is not Dean Burgon's way of changing the Textus Receptus.

Don't go along with the so-called Majority Text Onlyism of either Hodges and Farstad or Robinson and Pierpoint. They have two different Majority Texts they are battling about.

<u>Let's take a look at the so-called Majority Text (or Byzantine Text as Price calls it) of Hodges and Farstad</u>. What have they done? If you look at their introduction of their Greek New Testament, based on Kurt Aland's 1967 total of 5,255 manuscripts available, you will see the following:

★   1.   Of the Greek <u>papyrus</u> fragments, they used only 8 out of 81 (10% of the evidence).

★   2.   Of the Greek <u>uncials</u>, they only picked out 4 out of 267 (1% of the evidence).

★   3.   Of the Greek <u>cursives</u>, they only used 414 out of 2,764 (15% of the evidence).

★   4.   Of the Greek <u>lectionaries</u>, they used 0 out of 2,143 (0% of the evidence).

★   5.   Of the Greek <u>total manuscripts</u> they used 426 out of 5,255 (8% of the evidence).

★   6.   Of the many Greek <u>ancient versions</u> they used 0 out of 20 (0% of the evidence).

★   7.   Of the Greek '<u>Church Fathers</u>' over 86,000 quotations or allusions, they used 0 (0% of the evidence).

Now, let's examine Price's Greek text that he uses as we have examined Price's so-called "***Byzantine text***" or the so-called "***Majority text***." **It is the Nestle/Aland Greek Text (26ᵗʰ and 27ᵗʰ edition).** If you look at their introduction, here is what you find for the so-called Nestle/Aland Text that James Price worships against the Textus Receptus that underlies our King James Bible.

✓   1.   Of the Greek <u>papyrus</u> fragments, they used 81 out of 81 (100% of the evidence).

✓   2.   Of the Greek <u>uncials</u>, they used 246 out of 267 (92% of the evidence).

✓ 3. Of the Greek <u>cursives</u>, they used only 202 out of 2,764 (7% of the evidence).

✓ 4. Of the Greek <u>lectionaries</u>, they used only 5 out of 2,143 (0.23% of the evidence).

✓ 5. Of the Greek <u>total manuscripts</u> they used 534 out of 5,255 (10% of the evidence).

✓ 6. Of the many Greek <u>ancient versions</u> they used 3 out of 20 (15% of the evidence).

✓ 7. Of the Greek <u>Church Fathers</u> over 86,000 quotations or allusions, they used 72 quotations out of 200 (24 % of the evidence).

The grand total of all the evidence for the Nestle/Aland false Gnostic Greek text is 609 out of 5,255 or only 11% of all the evidence.

That is what Price wants us to believe is the Scripture? This is not the method that Dean John William Burgon insisted on. He wanted 100% of the evidence to be used, otherwise, just leave the Greek text alone as the Textus Receptus which has come down to us from Apostolic times.

# Burgon Not A KJB-Only Ruckmanite

**STATEMENT #17.** (p. 12) *"Technically it is true that Cloud listed Burgon among those who opposed the Revised Standard Version, but he never clearly distinguishes Burgon's Traditional Text from the Textus Receptus, and he leaves the readers the impression that Burgon supports a King James Only view."*

**COMMENT #17.** Regarding Dean Burgon's identification of the "*Received*" text with the "*Traditional Greek Text*," as I have quoted above, he wrote "*call it the–'Received,' or the Traditional Greek Text, or whatever other name you please*" (Dean Burgon, *The Revision Revised*, p. 269). Here again, in quoting Cloud, Price identifies his "*King James Only*" smear term with the Peter Ruckman position. Though Dean Burgon stood firmly for the King James Bible, it is totally false to assume for one moment that he was a "*Ruckmanite/King James Only*" as Price has used this term in referring to Cloud's statement. This is a terri`ble slander by Price on those of us who stand, as Dean Burgon did, for the King James Bible and the underlying Hebrew, Aramaic, and Greek Words.

# I Hold To Words Underlying the KJB

**STATEMENT #18.** (p. 16) Price has the following heading: "*Some insist on the Textus Receptus underlying the King James Version*," Then he wrote: "*Some Christians use only the King James Version for the reasons* *listed above, but also because it was translated from a particular form of the Textus Receptus--the Hebrew and Greek words behind the English words of the King James Version.*"

**COMMENT #18.** For many years, Price and other of his friends who use the Gnostic critical Greek text (of either Westcott and Hort, Nestle/Aland, or United Bible Societies) have made fun of Textus Receptus people. They asked these people which of the many Textus Receptus Greek texts they follow, because there are many going by that name. To make it easier on these detractors, I, and others, have showed them the exact Textus Receptus that I hold to be the original preserved Greek New Testament Words. The Textus Receptus that I am holding to consists of the Words "*underlying the King James Version.*" The same goes for the Old Testament Hebrew and Aramaic Words. They are those Words "*behind the English words of the King James Version.*" This is simply a needed definition of terms so Price and others know exactly what we are talking about.

# Price's False Ruckmanite Smear

**STATEMENT #19.** (p. 17)   Price wrote: "*I include Hills, Ray, Fuller, Waite, Cloud and their followers in this category. . . . Therefore it is the English words that determine the Hebrew and Greek text, not the Hebrew and Greek words that determine the English text. Consequently, I see no practical difference between this view and that of Peter Ruckman who openly declares that the King James English corrects the Hebrew and Greek.*"

**COMMENT #19.** Price's twisting of truth and slander is clearly seen here. He sees "*no practical difference between this view and that of Peter Ruckman who openly declares that the King James English corrects the Hebrew and Greek.*" It is certainly **not** true that "*English words*" are those that "*determine the Hebrew and Greek text.*" Price is saying that the King James Bible translators "*back-translated*" their selected English words into the Hebrew, Aramaic, and Greek languages. This stupidity and ignorance of the facts and logic is unbecoming from such a well-trained and intelligent gentleman and scholar. The plain fact is that the King James Bible translators had Traditional Hebrew, Aramaic, and Greek Words before them that they translated into English. As far as identifying me and the four other men with the heretical teachings of Peter Ruckman "*who openly declares that the King James English corrects the Hebrew and Greek.*" I challenge Price to produce a single quotation from me or any of the other four men to the effect "*that the King James English corrects the Hebrew and Greek.*" Price cannot do this because such quotations do not exist. As a Christian gentleman, he should immediately write an apology to me and the other four men for this demeaning falsehood.

# Price's Definition of King James Only

**STATEMENT #20.** (p. 18) "*Finally in these last days English has become the international language, consequently God providentially guided a translation of the Bible into English–the King James Version of 1611. Today this Bible is the __inspired, infallible, inerrant__ Word of God preserved for the English-speaking world.*"

**COMMENT #20.** This is Price's definition of King James Only. I do not use the words "*__inspired, infallible, inerrant__*." Many of the others of us who stand responsibly for the King James Bible do not use these three words for a "*__translation__*," even the King James Bible, but many do. These words are rightly applied only for the original and preserved Hebrew, Aramaic, and Greek Words underlying the King James Bible. I think it is Ruckmanite heresy to believe that in 1611 God "*__breathed out__*" or '*__inspired__*" the words of the King James Bible. This action by God occurred only once and that was when He "*__breathed out__*" the original Hebrew, Aramaic, and Greek Words. It was never repeated by God. It does not take place in any translation. To say that it does is what I term as a heresy. This is the heresy of Peter Ruckman who believes that God "*__breathed out__*" or "*__inspired__*" the King James Bible as a "*__revelation from God__*" rather than a translation by sinful men.

As far as the words "*__infallible__*" and "*__inerrant__*," I cannot use these absolute terms for the King James Bible or any translation by men. To say that the King James Bible is "*__infallible and inerrant__*," I would have to use these words for the erroneous and false Apocrypha which the King James Bible translators foolishly included in their 1611 edition. This was a terrible disgrace for the King James translators to put in that heretical section into the 1611 translation of the Bible. Many of the early editions of the King James Bible were loaded with printing errors, some of which were quite serious and even wicked.

**STATEMENT #21.** (p. 18) "*The last two views above are what I regard as radical __King James Onlyism__.*"

**COMMENT #21.** The "*__last two views__*" he refers to are as follows: (1) "*__Some insist on the Textus Receptus underling the King James Version__*," and (2) "*__Some insist on the King James Version only__*." Though the last position is Ruckmanism, the position before that is my position and many others who hold to the original and preserved Hebrew, Aramaic, and Greek Words underlying the King James Bible as the foundation of Bible truth. What

Price has just said is a vicious slander on my position, tying me into "*Ruckmanism/King James Onlyism*" which is totally false.

# Text Not Preserved by "Bibles"

**STATEMENT #22.** (p. 19) "*The important doctrine of textual preservation is discussed in Chapter 7, describing the various proposed theories of how the Biblical text has been preserved down through history. I conclude that the text has been preserved in the consensus of the Bibles that have survived from antiquity....*"

> **COMMENT #22.** This is a pitiful definition of "*textual preservation*" and Price should know better. Bible preservation consists of the preservation of the original Hebrew, Aramaic, and Greek *Words* and certainly not in the "*consensus of the Bibles that have survived.*" It is his false emphasis on "*translations*" for "*textual preservation*" rather than on the preserved original Hebrew, Aramaic, and Greek Words.

# Eight Modern English Versions

**STATEMENT #23.** (p. 20) Price is now talking about comparing "*eight modern English versions*" with the King James Version. It includes "*Their teachings on seven of the cardinal doctrines of Evangelical Fundamental theology. (1) the Deity of Christ. (2) the virgin birth of Christ. (3) The atonement by the blood of Christ. (4) justification by faith. (5) the bodily resurrection of Christ. (6) the second coming of Christ, and (7) the doctrine of salvation.*"

**COMMENT #23.** Price is implying that these "*eight modern English versions*" (based as they are on the false Gnostic-contaminated Nestle/Aland 26th edition) are doctrinally sound. This is absolutely false. Dr. Jack Moorman has written an excellent book called, *Early Manuscripts, Church Fathers, and the Authorized Version.* It is **BFT #3230** @ $20.00 + $5.00 S&H. On pages 119-312, Dr. Moorman identifies over 356 doctrinal passages where the New International Version (NIV), by following their Gnostic-contaminated Critical Texts, has erred from sound doctrine.

# Price's Denial of Doctrinal Change

**STATEMENT #24.** (p. 20) Price is talking about various original language texts when they might differ. "*In any case, the alternatives do not affect the overall teaching of Biblical truth and doctrine.*"

**COMMENT #24.** This is false. He is bearing false witness against truth. He is saying that in all of these "*eight modern English versions*" which are based on the Gnostic Critical Text (which he himself favors) "*do not affect the overall teaching of Biblical truth and doctrine*." As I mentioned in **COMMENT #23** above, the "*overall teaching of Biblical truth and doctrine*" is affected in "*over 356 doctrinal passages*." Each one of these 356 doctrines are detailed in Dr. Jack Moorman's book, *Early Manuscripts, Church Fathers, and the Authorized Version*, pages 119-312. It is **BFT** #3230 @ $20.00 + $5.00 S&H. When Price wrote that "*the alternatives do not affect the overall teaching of Biblical truth and doctrine*." it is a blatant falsehood.

# False Date of Septuagint (LXX)

**STATEMENT #25.** (pp. 21-22) Price's chapter title is "*Early English Versions were Incomplete Until Wycliffe*." Price wrote: "*In the meanwhile, a large colony of Jews had settled in Alexandria, Egypt and adopted the Greek language. About the second or third Century B.C., they translated the Hebrew Bible into the Greek to accommodate their worship in the Synagogue. This Greek translation of the Old Testament became known as the Septuagint.*"

**COMMENT #25.** Neither Price nor any other person has solid documentary and irrefutable evidence that "*they translated the Hebrew Bible into the Greek,*" the entire Bible from Genesis to Malachi, in the "*second or third Century B.C.,*" or any other century B.C. Though there are a few books, that can be proved to be B. C., no man on earth can produce a B.C. copy of the entire Old Testament in Greek. Yes, he can produce a few books that were in Greek B.C., but not the entire Old Testament. If Price can produce a copy of this, let him call me up at 856-854-4747 and invite me at a satisfactory time and place for me to come over and see it. I'll bring my video camera and tape recorder to record the entire meeting. If he cannot produce it, he (and his entire group of Fundamental friends) should stop saying this. This so-called Septuagint was produced in Greek from Genesis through Malachi in the time of Origen (c. 185 to 254). It is the 5th column of Origen's six-column Hexapla.

# The KJB Translators' Ability

**STATEMENT #26.** (p. 72). Under the caption of "*The Qualifications of the Translators,*" Price wrote: "*Undoubtedly, the men selected as translators were highly qualified for the work. Some King James Only advocates have gone so far as to claim that there has never been such a highly qualified group of translators either before or since.*"

**COMMENT #26.** Though I am not one of Price's "*King James Only*" Ruckmanite people, I agree that "*there has never been such a highly qualified group of translators either before or since*" the time of the King James translators. To have Price think that he (though with high qualifications) and his cohorts have anywhere near the qualifications of these men is totally erroneous and even egomaniacal. Price can't hold a candle to Hebraists on the translation team of the King James Bible. In my book, *Defending the King James Bible* (**BFT #1594 @ $12.00 + $5.00 S&H**), the entire third chapter deals with the superior linguistics of the King James Bible translators. This is one of the reasons why the King James Bible is a superior English translation.

# Details of KJB Translators' Abilities

**STATEMENT #27.** (p. 76) "*Thus, while the academic skills of the KJV translators may be admired for their great achievements, there is no reason to suppose that they were, on the whole, more highly qualified than those who preceded or followed them. Every generation has its exceptional linguists, and theologians and every generation builds on the foundation left by their predecessors.*"

**COMMENT #27.** For Price to say "*there is no reason to suppose that they were, on the whole, more highly qualified than those who preceded or followed them*" is tremendously false. He is trying to push himself and his friends who are "*Critical Text Onlyists*" as being higher scholars than the King James Bible translators.

Let's take a look at the accomplishments of three of these early Old Testament translators and two New Testament translators. The following section is taken directly from my book, *Defending the King James Bible*, [BFT #1594 @ $12.00 + $4.00 S&H] pages 67-75:

### THREE SUPERIOR KING JAMES
### OLD TESTAMENT TRANSLATORS.

✦    1.    **The Accomplishments of Lancelot Andrews. First we will consider the Old Testament translators of the King James Bible and the accomplishments of Dr. Lancelot Andrews. He was the president or director of the Westminster group that translated twelve books altogether, from Genesis to 2 Kings. That was the task of Company One.**

✓    a.    **First of all, he acquired most of the modern languages of Europe at the University of Cambridge. He gave himself chiefly to the Oriental tongues and to divinity [this is from *Translators Revived* [BFT #1419 @ $13.00 + $5.00 S&H] by**

Alexander McClure, p. 78].

✓    b.    Second, Lancelot Andrews' manual for his private devotions, prepared by himself, is wholly in the Greek language. You can see the man was accomplished. Many Christians today don't even have private daily devotions. Of those who do, how many do you know who have made up private devotions manuals? And of the people who have made up private devotions manuals, how many do you know who have written them wholly in the Greek language? This most certainly indicates a linguistic superiority. [ *op. cit.*, p. 86]

✓    c.    Third, "Such was his skill in all languages, especially the Oriental, that had he been present at the confusion of tongues at Babel, he might have served as *interpreter-general.*" [*op. cit.*, p. 86] That is a great statement, isn't it?

✓    d.    Fourth, "In his funeral sermon by Dr. Buckeridge, Bishop of Rochester, it is said that Dr. Andrews was conversant with "fifteen languages." [*op. cit.*, p. 87] Certainly he was a respected and superior translator. I don't know of any of these modern translators of the American Standard Version, New American Standard Version, New International Version, New English Version, etc. who are conversant with as many as fifteen languages, do you?

✦    2.    The Acumen of William Bedwell. Dr. William Bedwell was also in Company One, the Westminster group translating the books of Genesis through 2 Kings from the Hebrew into the English. Let us note a few things about him:

✓    a.    First, he was justly reputed to be "an eminent Oriental scholar."

✓    b.    Second, his fame for Arabic learning was so great that scholars sought him out for assistance. To him belongs, as McClure stated:

> *"the honor of being the first who considerably promot-ed and revived the study of the Arabic language and literature in Europe." [op. cit., p. 101]*

✓    c.    Third, in Antwerp, in 1612, he published in *quarto* an edition of the Epistles of St. John in Arabic with a Latin version. Now, I don't know anything about Arabic, but to have an edition of 1, 2, and 3rd John with Latin and Arabic would take a tremendously capable scholar, a capable builder of this building, the King James Bible.

✓    d.    Fourth, he also left many Arabic manuscripts in the University of Cambridge, with numerous notes
and a font of types for printing them.

✓    e.    Fifth, for many years he was engaged in
compiling an Arabic lexicon in three volumes [a lexicon is a
dictionary]. [*op. cit.*, pp. 100-101]

✓    f.    Sixth, as McClure wrote:

*"Some modern scholars [in 1857 when McClure wrote
his book] have fancied we have an advantage in our
times over the translators of the KING JAMES days of
1611 by reason of the greater attention which is
supposed to be paid at present [in 1857] to what are
called the 'COGNATE' and 'Shemitic' languages,
especially the Arabic, by which much light is thought to
be reflected on Hebrew words and phrases. It is evi-
dent, however, that Mr. Bedwell and others among his
fellow laborers, were THOROUGHLY CONVERSANT
in this part of the broad field of sacred criticism."*

✓    g.    Seventh, Dr. Bedwell also began a Persian
dictionary, which is among Archbishop Laud's manuscripts still
preserved in the Bodleian Library at Oxford. [*op. cit.*, pp. 101-
102]

This William Bedwell, with his Arabic, Persian, and other
Oriental languages, was a greatly superior translator to our
*modern translators*. Many modern "*translators*" come up to a
word, and in a footnote somewhere or in an index at the bottom
of the page, they'll say the meaning of this Hebrew word is
uncertain; so they have some other rendition of it. Well, the
meaning of it is uncertain, perhaps, to these men who were
living in 1960, when the NASV came out, in 1969, when the NIV
came out or in 1980, when the New King James came out; but
these men who translated the King James Bible knew their
cognate languages well. They understood these references and
there was no question in their minds about what most of these
words meant. It is a strange thing; yet people doubt and
question the authenticity, superiority, and the knowledge of
these King James Translators. Cognate languages are simply
sister languages related to Hebrew like Arabic, Persian, Syriac,
Aramaic, Coptic, and so on. They are related like brother and
sister.

A word may not be clear, or maybe the word is what they call a
*hapax legomenon*. *Hapax* means *"once"* and *legomenon* means *"spoken
or written."* This particular word was used only once in all the New
Testament Greek or Old Testament Hebrew. So it is difficult to tell
sometimes what these *hapax legomena* (in the plural) mean. They go to
other sources to try to understand the meaning. The translators of the
King James, who knew Arabic, Persian, Aramaic, Coptic, and all the
various cognate languages, could go to these languages and understand
very clearly. But the men living today, because they don't know these
cognate languages as well [they don't know fifteen languages like Andrews
for example], just throw up their hands and say the meaning of the
Hebrew is not certain.

✦     3.     The Acceptability of Miles Smith. Dr. Miles
Smith was in Company Three, the Oxford Group. That group
translated a total of seventeen books, from Isaiah through
Malachi. Here is some of the background on Dr. Smith:

✓     a.     First, he was one of the twelve translators
selected to revise the work after it was referred to them for the
final examination.

✓     b.     Second, Dr. Smith was employed to write
that most learned and eloquent preface to the King James Bible.

✓     c.     Third, he went through the Greek and
Latin Fathers, making his annotations on them all. There were
100 Church Fathers that wrote extensively from 100 to 300 A.
D. There were 200 more who wrote from 300 to 600 A. D. He
read through all of them in Greek and Latin and made his own
comments on each of them.

✓     d.     Fourth, he was well acquainted with the
Rabbinical glosses and comments. These are marginal
comments in the Hebrew language.

✓     e.     Fifth, so expert was he in the Chaldee
(which is related to the Hebrew), the Syriac and the Arabic, that
they were almost as familiar as his native tongue.

✓     f.     Sixth, Hebrew, he had at his finger's ends.
An extremely proficient man, and certainly superior in his
qualifications to translate our King James Bible. [*op. cit.*, pp.
141-43]

## TWO SUPERIOR KING JAMES
## NEW TESTAMENT TRANSLATORS.

Let us take a look at the superiority of two of the New Testament translators of the King James Bible.

✦   1.   The Activities of Henry Savile. Sir Henry Savile was in Company Four, the Oxford group. That group had the task of translating six books: the Gospels, Acts, and Revelation. Here is some of the background on Henry Savile:

✓   a.   First, he became, very early, famous for his Greek and mathematical learning.

✓   b.   Second, he became tutor in Greek and Mathematics to Queen Elizabeth.

✓   c.   Third, he translated the histories of Cornelius Tacitus and published the same with notes. Tacitus was a Latin historian, and Savile translated his work into English.   The translators of these new versions, I'm sure, wouldn't be able to translate anything this complicated in Latin. In our country, Latin used to be required in the lower grades. In many schools it was a requirement for graduation from High School. Years ago that was the case; but now, in some schools, you don't have to take any foreign language at all. Some require you to take one--maybe French, German or Spanish. I took a year of Latin in college, but didn't have to take it in High School. I took Spanish there, and French in college. Of course I studied Hebrew and Greek in Seminary.

✓   d.   Fourth, Henry Savile published, from the manuscripts, the writings of *Bradwardin against Pelagius*, the *Writers of English History Subsequent to Bede*, and *Prelections on the Elements of Euclid*. Euclid was concerned with geometry and wrote in Greek. Savile translated that, and other learned works in English and Latin.   He certainly had to have tremendous skill in order to do so. Some of the works in Greek are most difficult.

✓   e.   Fifth, he is chiefly known, however, for being the first to edit the complete work of Chrysostom, the most famous of the Greek Fathers. John Chrysostom had many pages that he wrote to the people to whom he ministered, and Savile was the first to completely edit his work. His edition of 1,000 copies was made in 1613, and makes eight immense folios. A folio is the size of a large dictionary or encyclopedia. That was a monumental task. I don't know any of the modern translators of the new versions (or perversions) who come anywhere near the superiority and skill of this man.

    ✓    f.    Sixth, Sir Henry Savile was one of the most profound, exact, and critical scholars of his age and "meet and ripe" [as McClure noted] to take a part in the preparation of our incomparable version. [cf. McClure's *Translators Revived*, [BFT #1419 @ $13.00 + $5.00 S&H], pp. 164-69].

    ✦    2.    The Academics of John Bois. One more New Testament translator, John Bois, was in Company Six, the Cambridge group, which translated all the books of the Apocrypha.

# Apocrypha Is Not the Word of God

    ✓    a.    Why We Do Not Accept the Apocrypha. Since we have brought up the Apocrypha, the doubtful books, that the Roman Catholic Church has added to their Old Testament, I want to repeat that the Church of England in their *Thirty-Nine Articles*, clearly stated that the Apocrypha had no Scriptural standing. It is not the Words of God. It is not inspired. But the 1611 King James Bible did contain the Apocrypha. They translated it as history between the Old and New Testaments. Modern versions of the King James do not use the Apocrypha. Let me quote from McClure's, *Translators Revived--Biographical Notes on the KJB Translators*, [ BFT #1419 @ $13.00 + $5.00 S&H] concerning the Apocrypha.

> [Page 185]: *"The sixth and last company of KING JAMES BIBLE translators met in Cambridge. To this company was assigned all the Apocryphal books, which, in those times were more read and accounted of than now, though by no means placed on a level with the canonical books of Scripture."*

Then there's a footnote:

> *"The reasons assigned for not admitting the Apocryphal books into the canon, or list of inspired Scriptures are briefly the following:*
>
>     *✦ 1. Not one of them is in the Hebrew language, which was alone used by the inspired historians and poets*

of the Old Testament. [All but one are in Greek. The other one is in Latin].

✦ *2. Not one of the writers lays any claim to inspiration.* [Not one says, "The Lord spoke through me," or "These are the words of God."]

✦ *3. These books were never acknowledged as sacred Scriptures by the Jewish Church, and therefore were never sanctioned by our Lord.*

✦ *4. They were not allowed a place among the sacred books during the first four centuries of the Christian Church.*

✦ *5. They contain fabulous statements* [in the sense of being fables] *and statements which contradict not only the canonical Scripture but themselves; as when in the two books of Maccabees Antiochus Epiphanes is made to die three different deaths in as many different places.*

✦ *6. It inculcates doctrines at variance with the Bible, such as prayers for the dead,* [that is why the Roman Catholic Church prays for the dead] *and sinless perfection.*

✦ *7. It teaches immoral practices, such as lying* [it couldn't be the Words of God and say it's okay to lie], *suicide, assassination and magical incantations.* [God is against that in His Words--necromancers, those with familiar spirits, and wizards that "peep," as the Bible says, all are forbidden in Scripture].

*For these and other reasons, the Apocryphal books which are all in Greek, except one which is extant only in Latin, are valuable only as ancient documents, illustrative of the manners, language, opinions and history of the East."* [My words in brackets].

✓    b.    Background of John Bois.

✦    (1)    First, John Bois was carefully taught by his father. That is a good thing, isn't it? Fathers should teach more things to their children instead of leaving it up to the schools or Sunday School teacher. Talk about a child prodigy-- at the age of five years he had read the Bible–in Hebrew. Think what kind of people in our day have anything even approaching the background of this man, John Bois. These men were giants compared to the scholarly "pygmies" walking the earth today. The reason it makes me provoked is that men are ridiculing the King James Bible as being old fashioned, outdated, inadequate, inferior--heaping up adjectives against this precious Book. They say the King James Bible translators were inferior and didn't have the privilege of all the learning we have today. The truth is absolutely the reverse. We don't have the privilege of all the learning that they had. Ask if any of the translators of the modern versions have read the Bible through at the age of five! They probably couldn't even read at five. Then put those other two words on the end--"in Hebrew" and see what they say to that. They probably won't believe you. But this is found in McClure's book, *Translators Revived* [ BFT #1419 @ $13.00 + $5.00 S&H], (p. 200).

✦    (2)    Second, by the time Bois was six years old he not only wrote Hebrew legibly but in a fair and elegant character. If any of you know anything about Hebrew, it's not always easy to make the letters. He was writing them in a fair and elegant character at the age of six. [*Translators Revived* [ BFT #1419 @ $13.00 + $5.00 S&H], p. 200].

✦ (3) Third, he soon distinguished himself by his great skill in Greek, writing letters in that language to the Master and Senior Fellows at his college. If you know anything about the Greek language, you don't usually write letters in Greek. It's difficult enough to translate from the Greek into the English without composing letters, or talking in New Testament, or Classical Greek. This man was a skilled man, not only in the Hebrew but also in the Greek. [*Translators Revived* [ BFT #1419 @ $13.00 + $5.00 S&H], p. 200].

✦ (4) Fourth, in the chambers of Dr. Downe, the chief university lecturer in the Greek language, Bois read with him twelve Greek authors in prose--the hardest that could be found both for dialect and phrase. It was a common practice for this young man to read and study in the University Library at four a.m. and stay without intermission until eight in the evening, a total of sixteen hours straight. [ *op. cit.*, p. 201]

> The Classical Greek language has a number of divisions as far as its history. You go way back in the early Greek and you have the Homeric Greek. I studied Homeric Greek while majoring in Classical Greek and Latin at the University of Michigan. We studied Homer's *Iliad* and *Odyssey*. Now that is an entirely different Greek and hard to understand. Then Classical Greek is a little different in spelling, dialect, rules, and grammar. The Classical Greek had Ionic, Doric, and Attic. The Attic Greek was the branch that became what we call the Koine Greek. But before that was the Byzantine Greek. The Septuagint Greek was Koine Greek. The Koine period was roughly from 300 B. C. to 300 A. D. The Koine Greek, the common Greek, used in everyday language, was the Greek of the New Testament. Then we have modern Greek which is somewhat different and pronounced differently. But Bois used the Classical Greek and had twelve of the hardest authors in prose and poetry.

I remember when I studied Classical Greek at the University of Michigan. I was first of all majoring in Science and Math and was in the Pre-Medical major, intending to be a medical doctor. Then the Lord called me to His service, and changed my direction. I had to go to Seminary, so I changed my major. The seminary I was intending to enter (Dallas Theological Seminary), at that time, required eight hours of Greek before you could enter. So I majored in Greek and Latin, taking thirty hours between them. Before that, I had not had any language at all of a technical nature. I knew Spanish, but Greek was difficult at first. I took the beginning Classical Greek and took the advanced Classical Greek from Dr. Warren E. Blake who was head of the Classical Department at the University of Michigan at Ann Arbor. He was a scholar and very competent in his understanding of the Greek language. I remember we had to translate various authors in Attic Greek, especially Plato's *Apology*, the life of Socrates which told how he would refute all those who would argue with him. It was difficult Greek! I would look at English translations and then look at the Greek. The trouble was the translations weren't literal translations like the King James Bible is, so it was hard to figure out what the Greek was actually saying.

I remember many a time the professor would give a deep sigh as I was trying to translate, making no sense whatever out of the Greek words, but I did the best I could. So I think of John Bois, and twelve of the most difficult authors his teacher could find as Bois went flying successfully through them.

✦    (5)    Fifth, John Bois' library contained one of the most complete and costly collections of Greek literature that had ever been made. So, he was not only skilled as to his ability, but also had an extensive library to go with it. [*Translators Revived* [ BFT #1419 @ $13.00 + $5.00 S&H], p. 203].

✦    (6)    Sixth, he was equally distinguished for his skill in Greek and Hebrew.

✦    (7)    Seventh, he was one of the twelve translators who were sent, two from each company, to make the final revision at Stationer's Hall in London. This lasted nine months. If there were a problem in Hebrew or Greek, he had the answers.

✦    (8)    Eighth, he took notes of all the proceedings of this committee. He was the secretary. His notes, by the way, are some of the only evidences we have today telling us how they went about things. [*Translators Revived* [ BFT #1419 @ $13.00 + $5.00 S&H], p. 204].

✦    (9)   Ninth, he left at his death as many leaves of manuscript as he had lived days in his long life. I looked up his age, and he lived eighty-three years and eleven days. That totals 30,306 days. Imagine leaving over 30,000 pages of writing.  A voluminous writer, scholar, reader, and worker.

✦    (10)  Tenth, he was so familiar with the Greek Testament that he could, at any time, turn to any word that it contained. [*Translators Revived* [ BFT #1419 @ $13.00 + $5.00 S&H], pp. 199-208]."

So we have some translators here that certainly are superior by any standard you can think of or imagine. For the other translators, consult BFT #1419, #584, or #804 referred to above. We never need to be ashamed of the men who gave us the King James Bible.  They were skilled builders, building on the proper foundation with every tool at their disposal. They knew English, Greek, Hebrew, and the cognate sister languages. They applied their skills and did the job in a superior fashion.

If Price can give me the names of any of these Critical Text translators that have left 30,000 pages of published writings bring them on.   The translators of our King James Bible were scholars and geniuses in their time. These men today cannot compete with those who gave us our King James Bible. I am just simply saying that Price should not boast saying that he and his other translators have had more semester hours than the King James translators.  So, to have them boast and say that they are superior to our King James Bible translators, where is their humility?  This statement of Price is absolute folly.

# Some Greek Typos

**STATEMENT #28.**   (p.76)  "*. . . translating the Greek word (episkopos) as bishop rather than overseer, in their transliterating the Greek word (baptizo) as baptize rather than translating it as immerse, and so forth.*"

**COMMENT #28.**  The *Greek words* for "*bishop*" and for "*baptize*" were misprinted in the book.  This is no doubt a mistake in the printing of the book that was not checked well enough.  It is a minor point and is understandable how this has slipped through the editors.

# Translators' Theological Views

**STATEMENT #29.**  (p. 78)  "*It seems strange then to read of present-day Evangelicals and Fundamentalists who praise the theological* *views and spiritual discernment of the KJV translators as somehow being superior of that of any translator today.*"

> **COMMENT #29.** In the previous **COMMENT #27,** I have presented some of the superior linguistic qualifications of the King James Bible translators, BUT I HAVE NEVER SAID that their "*theological views and spiritual discernment*" are "*superior of that of any translator today.*" I am an independent Baptist who follows the Bible in all matters of doctrine. I am by no means in accord with many of the "*theological views*" of the Church of England to which the King James Bible translators belonged. I have no knowledge of their "*spiritual discernment,*" either good or bad.

# Translators' Piety and Character

**STATEMENT #30.** (p. 78). "*Some advocates of the King James Only view venerate the piety and godly character of the King James translators as being far superior to that of the translators of modern versions.*"

**COMMENT #30.** I don't talk about or "*venerate the piety and godly character*" of the King James translators. Though I don't question either their "*piety*" or "*godly character,*" I talk about the most important skill-- their ability, as translators, to translate.

# KJB Not A "Revision"

**STATEMENT #31.** (p. 82) "*The King James Version was a revision of the Bishops' Bible, not a new translation.*"

**COMMENT #31.** I don't agree with that at all. The translators were divided into six companies. In each of these three companies, there was an Old Testament and a New Testament section. They met in three different cities in England to put out this new translation. Though they compared the Bishops' Bible, the Great Bible, the Geneva Bible, the Tyndale Bible, and the other Bibles then available, it does not qualify as being merely a "*revision.*" This was a translation from the original Hebrew, Aramaic, and Greek languages. They called it a "*translation.*" They agree here and there with some other version, but I believe it must still be called a "*translation,*" not a "*revision.*"

# The Apocrypha in the KJB

**STATEMENT #32.** (p. 83) Price's heading here is "*The First Printing Was in 1611.*" Under this heading, he wrote: "*Like its predecessor, the 1611 version included the Apocrypha between the Old and New*

Testaments. *But unlike its predecessors that clearly stated the Apocrypha Books were not part of the Canon of Scripture, the 1611 version contained no comments about the canonicity of the Apocrypha, thus leaving the question open.*"

**COMMENT #32.** I side with the Puritans on this issue and wish that *the Apocrypha books* had never been included in the King James Bible. However, Article VI of the *39 Articles of the Church of England* does not list the Apocrypha Books as a part of the *Canonical Books* of Scripture. Despite this, the King James Bible translators were definitely to be faulted in including the Apocrypha in the 1611 edition. At least they put them between Malachi and Matthew rather than to intersperse them within the canonical books as the Roman Catholic and other versions have done.

# King James Only Smear Again

**STATEMENT #33.**  (p. 84)  "*The Anglican and the Episcopal Churches, as well as the English speaking Greek Orthodox Churches, use the Authorized Version containing the Apocrypha. Supporters of the King James Only view tend to ignore the fact that the Apocrypha is an official part of the Authorized Version.*"

**COMMENT #33.** As I have said before in this book, I am **NOT** one of the "*supporters of the King James Only view.*" That is why I must insist that Price has done me, and others who believe as I do, a gigantic disservice by throwing us into the "*King James Only*" false position. Since the Apocrypha is filled with doctrinal and other errors, it is nonsensical to maintain, as do the Peter Ruckman followers, that the King James Bibles was "*God-breathed,*" or "*inspired by God,*" or "*inspired.*" That makes God the Author of evil.

# Quoting Apostate Luther Weigle

**STATEMENT #34.** (p. 84) Price quotes apostate Luther Weigle without warning his readers of his apostasy. Price quoted: "*For eighty years after its publication in 1611, the King James version endured bitter attacks. It was denounced as theologically unsound . . .*"

**COMMENT #34.**  Weigle is talking about the Geneva Bible and bashing the King James Bible. Price is using this apostate to condemn the King James Bible. I think he could get enough of his Fundamental Bible believing friends to support his arguments against that Bible rather than to stoop to using an avowed apostate, especially without warning his readers of the apostasy of <u>Luther Weigle</u>.

# KJB Departures From 1611 Edition

**STATEMENT #35.** (p. 91) This is from Price's Chapter 5 entitled: "*The King James Version was Revised Several Times.*" Price wrote: "*Numberless and not inconsiderable <u>departures from the original</u> or standard Authorized Version as published in 1611, are to be found...*"

> **COMMENT #35.** He is quoting Scrivener, but he did not define "*numberless*" and "*not inconsiderable <u>departures</u>.*" In the almost 800,000 words in the King James Bible, aside from spelling and punctuation changes, there is a very small number of changes. In <u>listening</u>, I <u>heard</u> a little over 400 examples. Another man <u>looked at</u> the changes and came up with 2,000, but when I examined each of these, I found there to be only about 1,000 differences. Whether 400, 1,000, or even 2,000, this is a tiny percentage of the almost 800,000 words.

# KJB's Readability

**STATEMENT #36.** (p. 99) Price wrote: "*As a result, English language usage has drifted quite far from that of the 1769 King James Version, and <u>most people find this version difficult to read and to understand</u>.*"

**COMMENT #36.** If indeed, as Price believes that "<u>*most people find this version difficult to read and to understand*</u>." he should urge his friends to read the *Defined King James Bible* published by the **Bible For Today** ministry. This Bible defines very clearly, in the footnotes, any uncommon words in the King James Bible. There is no problem understanding the version. In fact, my high school janitor who never got through the 5th grade, and led me to Christ understood the King James Bible without a problem. What's wrong with our educational system today? We've been dumbed down as they say.

As far as readability is concerned, Price should read D. A. Waite, Jr.'s excellent booklet entitled *The Comparative Readability of the Authorized Version* (**BFT #2671** @ $6.00 + $3.00 S&H). The author compares the KJB with six other versions (ASV, RSV, NASV, NIV, NKJV, & NRSV). Based on sound and current standards of readability, he found the King James Bible to be more readable in most areas based on these well established standards.

# Not 24,000 Vital Changes Made

**STATEMENT #37.** (p. 99)  Price had this distorted and very misleading heading. "_Nearly 24,000 Changes Were Made_." He is comparing the present King James Bible with the original AV of 1611.

**COMMENT #37.** When Price proclaims that "_Nearly 24,000 Changes Were Made_" in the original King James Bible, he implies that these are substantial and important changes.  I discount spelling and punctuation changes as not significant "_changes_."  For example, in the AV 1611 the word "_sin_" was spelled, "_SINNE_."  Spelling differences are not significant "changes" and should not be included in Price's alleged _24,000_ total.  That had to be changed to SIN.  If you want to call that a change it is a minor change.  In my study, _KJB/1611 Compared to KJB/1769_ (**BFT #1294** @ **$2.00 + $1.00 S&H**), I found to the ear, some 427 small changes that I could hear.  Another gentleman used his eyes rather than his ears and came up with 2,000 small changes of words.  I analyzed his research and cut his total to only about 1,000 small changes of words.  Even if there are 1,000 or even 2,000 small changes, what is that among nearly 800,000 words in the King James Bible?  This is a long way from "_24,000 Changes_."

# The Message Versus the Words

**STATEMENT #38.** (p. 99)  "_With the number of revisions that have been made to the 1611 edition, it is important to consider the extent of the changes and their effect on the purity of the **divine message**._"

**COMMENT #38.** Price is concerned only about the "_divine message_," I am concerned about the "_divine Words_." This is the slippery slope of those, like Price, who do not believe in plenary verbal preservation of the Hebrew, Aramaic and Greek Words. These people get into the inferior talk about only the "_message_" of the Bible rather than its "_Words_." These small "changes" are the most minor possible. To see some of them, look over my BFT #2.50 + $2.00 S&H.

# Changes Inconsequential

**STATEMENT #39.** (p. 103)  "_These examples make it clear that the factual details of **the divine message** were affected to some degree by the changes made by the revisers. . . . Such discrepancies were **usually inconsequential, not influencing doctrine and truth**._"

**COMMENT #39.** If indeed these small changes were "_usually inconsequential, not influencing doctrine and truth_," why is Price making so much of this matter? His "*24,000*" number is in error at the outset because he is including spelling, though he implies the changes were more serious. I would be interested in seeing all of his alleged "*24,000*" to see just how he can come up to that number.

# Is It "Deception"?

**STATEMENT #40.** (p. 103) "*The current editions of the King James Versions differ significantly from the 1611 edition in words, phrases, and at times in meaning. Leading people to believe that the Bible they carry to church is the 1611 edition is nothing short of deception, deception that cannot be justified by pious rationalization.*"

**COMMENT #40.** For Price to scare people who use their King James Bibles today that "*nearly 24,000 changes were made,*" implying that these were serious, "*is nothing short of deception.*"

# Smear With Ruckman's Views

**STATEMENT #41.** (p. 122) Price's Chapter 6 was called "*Current Editions of the King James Version Differ.*" In view of this, he wrote: "*Therefore it would be wrong to dogmatically insist, apart from the authority of the Hebrew and Greek texts, that the King James Version is the verbally inspired, infallible, inerrant Word of God when it is known that the various current editions have verbal differences with variations of meaning.*"

**COMMENT #41.** I have observed that only Peter Ruckman and his followers state that "*the King James Version is the verbally inspired, infallible, inerrant Word of God.*" I have never said this, nor do I believe it. Only the Hebrew, Aramaic and Greek Words were "*verbally inspired*" and therefore "*infallible and inerrant.*" This is why I believe Price should have written a book against Ruckmanism rather than tying in those of us who oppose the Ruckman ideas and slandering us as "*King James Only*" or followers of Peter Ruckman. This is false and disgusting on Price's part.

# Two Kinds of Preservation

**STATEMENT #42.** (p. 122) "*Likewise, it is wrong to claim that the King James Version of the Bible is the providentially preserved English Bible, when it is known that the various editions of the King James Version differ one from the other from decade to decade, and from edition to edition, even to the present day.*"

**COMMENT #42.** I don't use the terms, "*providentially preserved English Bible*" for the King James Bible. I say that the Hebrew, Aramaic, and Greek Words underlying the King James Bible are the "*Preserved original Words of God.*" I say, with a small "p" that the King James Bible is God's Words "*preserved in English*" because of its accurate translation of the "*Preserved Hebrew, Aramaic, and Greek Words.*"

# Inerrancy Not Limited to Originals

**STATEMENT #43.** (p. 122) "*The doctrine of verbal inspiration and inerrancy is limited to the words that were written by the inspired prophets and apostles.*"

**COMMENT #43.** First of all I say that "*verbal inspiration*" is limited to the original Hebrew, Aramaic, and Greek Words, but "*inerrancy*" is not so limited. Contrary to Price, I believe that "*inerrancy*" is not limited to the original Hebrew, Aramaic, and Greek Words, but is also found in those Preserved Traditional Hebrew, Aramaic, and Greek Words underlying the King James Bible.

# Prophets & Apostles Not "Inspired"

**STATEMENT #44.** (p. 122) In this context, Price talked about "… the *words that were written by the inspired prophets and apostles.*"

**COMMENT #44.** I believe it is heretical for Price to refer to "*inspired prophets and apostles.*" God did not "*inspire*" or "*breathe out*" either "*prophets or apostles.*" He "*inspired*" or "*breathed out*" His Hebrew, Aramaic, and Greek Words as 2 Timothy 3:16 clearly and unequivocally teaches. Price is dead wrong here. No prophet or apostle was ever "*inspired.*" It was his writings that were "*inspired*" or "*God-breathed*" (THEOPNEUSTOS as in 2 Timothy 3:16) God "*moved*" the "*apostles and prophets*" (2 Peter 1:21) but He did not "*inspire*" them.

# Preservation Not From Translations

**STATEMENT #45.** (p. 125) Price's Chapter 7 is entitled: "*The Biblical Text was Preserved through Ancient Bibles.*"

**COMMENT #45.** If Price is talking about the doctrine of Biblical preservation, Price is woefully in error. Price attended the Los Angeles Baptist Theological Seminary (p. 1 above). Is that where he got the heresy of "*inspired prophets and apostles*" and now Biblical preservation "*through ancient Bibles*"? This is absolutely false. "*The*"

> _Biblical text_" was preserved in the Hebrew, Aramaic, and Greek manuscripts, and not "through ancient Bibles." These "_ancient Bibles_" are "_translations_." The true, real, and genuine Bible is to be found in the original Hebrew, Aramaic, and Greek manuscripts rather than in any "_translation_," regardless of how close to those original languages they might be. Indeed, some of these "_ancient Bibles_" are founded on some of the wrong Hebrew, Aramaic, and Greek manuscripts, and may have any one or all of the following pitfalls:
>
>   (1) inferior translators,
>
>   (2) improper translation techniques, and
>
>   (3) heretical theology.

# Price Denies Verbal Preservation

**STATEMENT #46.** (p. 125) Price wrote: "_These passages primarily refer to certainty of fulfilled prophecy and the trustworthiness of Scripture_. Nevertheless one may infer from these passages that the Hebrew text of the Old Testament would be preserved on to the minutest detail. Referring to the New Testament to come after His resurrection, Jesus said, "Heaven and earth shall pass away, but my Words shall not pass away" ("_Matthew 24:35_"). Thus He anticipated the New Testament and its preservation."

**COMMENT #46.** Price is talking about two verses: (1) Luke 16:17 "_And it is easier for heaven and earth to pass, than one tittle of the law to fail._" and (2) Matthew 5:18 "_For verily I say unto you, Till heaven and earth pass, one jot or one tittle shall in no wise pass from the law, till all be fulfilled._" Price wrote that "_These passages primarily refer to certainty of fulfilled prophecy and the trustworthiness of Scripture_." This is absolutely false. These verses teach "_verbal Preservation_" of the originals. "_Matthew 5:18_" is a quotation of the Lord Jesus Christ as He proclaims the accurate "_plenary, verbal preservation_" of every letter and every punctuation mark of the Traditional Hebrew and Aramaic Old Testament Words (and, by extension, of the Traditional New Testament Greek Words as well).

# Prophets & Apostles Not "Inspired"

**STATEMENT #47.** Page 126, "_Obviously, the framers of the affirmation_ [this is the framers of the Westminster Confession of Faith] _meant the Hebrew and Greek words **God inspired the prophets and apostles to write**._"

> **COMMENT #47.** Price is in serious error when he repeats once again that "*God inspired the prophets and apostles to write*." He is misusing the word, "*inspired*." God did not inspire "*the prophets and apostles*" to write anything. They were "*moved*" (2 Peter 1:21), but not "*inspired.*" 2 Timothy 3:16 spells out clearly the meaning of Biblical "*inspiration*." This verse says "*All scripture is given by inspiration of God . . .*" The only thing that is "*given by inspiration of God*" (THEOPNEUSTOS or "*God-breathed*"), the only thing that is "*God-breathed*" or "*inspired*" is the "*scripture*" or the Words of God. God did not "*breathe out*" any of the "*prophets and apostles*," He breathed out WORDS. This is a false and heretical view of Biblical inspiration.

# Price's Heresy on Bible Preservation

**STATEMENT 48.** (p. 127) Price has a main heading with two paragraph headings that sound good, but that he really doubts. The main heading is: "*The text may have been preserved by various means.*" The two paragraph headings are: "*1. The autographs may have been preserved. 2. The text may have been preserved by perfect copies.*"

**COMMENT #48.** I rely on the Words of the Lord Jesus Christ being preserved until "*Heaven and earth*" pass away as He promised in three of the Gospels: "*Heaven and earth shall pass away, but my words shall not pass away*" (Matthew 24:35; Mark 13:31, and Luke 21:33). Though the exact physical "*autographs*" themselves may have "*passed away*," the **Words** that were written down on those "*autographs*" have not passed away, but have been preserved in the copies as our Saviour promised. He never breaks a promise!

**STATEMENT #49.** (p. 128) Price wrote: "3. *The text may have been preserved by* **imperfect copies**."

**COMMENT #49.** How can "*imperfect copies*" be a result of "*preservation*"? They would be the result of "*non-preservation*." How can Price twist the meanings of words this way? The text was not preserved if it is "*imperfect*." That is not preservation. I believe the original Words were preserved in the Traditional Hebrew, Aramaic, and Greek Words underlying the King James Bible. Price does not.

# The Source of Doctrinal Error

**STATEMENT #50.** (p. 128) "*Doctrinal error usually did not come about because of imperfections in the text of Scripture used in a particular time or place*, *but because of unbelief, faulty methods of interpretation, and the* *imposition of pagan philosophy.*"

**COMMENT #50.** It is totally false for Price to say that "*Doctrinal error usually did not come about because of imperfections in the text of Scripture used in a particular time or place*. Doctrinal error came into the Vatican and Sinai Gnostic manuscripts from Alexandria, Egypt, by these Gnostic heretics. These "*doctrinal errors*" came in the 4$^{th}$ Century B.C. when the Gnostic heretics succeeded in altering the original New Testament Words that they had received in over 8,000 places [See *8,000 Differences Between the Critical Text and the Traditional Text* by Dr. Jack Moorman **(BFT #3084 for a gift of $20.00 + $5.00 S&H)**]. This occurred in both the Vatican ("B") and Sinai (Aleph) manuscripts. Dean John William Burgon commented on how these early Gnostic heretics altered the Words of the originals:

> "*All that is intended by such statements is that these old heretics retained, altered, transposed, just so much as they pleased of the fourfold Gospel: and further, that they imported whatever additional matter they saw fit:--not that they rejected the inspired text entirely, and substituted something of their own invention in its place.*" (Dean John W. Burgon, *Causes of the Corruption of the Gospels*, p. 198)

> In other words, when these heretic Gnostics could not find the Words of the Bible to conform to their heresies, they changed those Words in order to make them conform. For this reason, in these Gnostic words of the Vatican and the Sinai manuscripts, there are over 356 doctrinal passages where doctrine is involved. For the details, consult the nearly 200 pages of documentation (pages 119-312) in *Early MSS, Church Fathers, & the Authorized Version* by Dr. Jack Moorman **(BFT #3230 for a gift of $20.00 + $5.00 S&H.)**

# 225 of His Statements and My Comments-- Statements ##51-100

## Confusion on Bible Preservation

**STATEMENT #51.** (p. 129) *"Some who hold to the King James Only view have been persuaded that the __autographic Hebrew and Greek texts of the Bible have not been preserved__, but rather that the current edition of the Authorized Version is the divinely preserved Scripture for this age."*

> **COMMENT #51.**  It is untrue to say that the *"__autographic Hebrew and Greek texts of the Bible have not been preserved__."* I believe that the original Hebrew, Aramaic, and Greek Words underlying the King James Bible are the *"__Preserved__"* original Words.  The King James Bible does not and cannot replace the *"__Preserved__"* original Hebrew, Aramaic, and Greek Words.  This is the totally false view of Peter Ruckman and his followers.  I do not believe that God breathed-out the King James Bible or any other translation.  This is pure and false Ruckmanism.

## The "Majority Text" Not Burgon's

**STATEMENT #52.** (p. 129)  In footnote #5 on this page, Price wrote: *"This view is known as __the Majority Text__. It originated with John W. Burgon, __The Traditional Text of the Holy Gospels Vindicated and Established__ rev. and edited by Edward Miller. . . ."*

**COMMENT #52.**  The present so-called *"__Majority Text__"* view was not the view of *"__John W. Burgon__."*  He wanted to have a Traditional Text established, but he did not do this in the *"__Majority Text__"* manner as Price implies. Dean Burgon called for the use of 100% of all of the evidence before arriving at any revision of the Received Text. However, the so-called "*Majority Text*" of Hodges and Farstad, failed miserably in this regard. They only used 10% of the papyri. Dean Burgon would have used 100%. They only used 1% of the uncials. Dean Burgon would have used 100% of them. They used only 15% of the cursive evidence. Dean Burgon would have used 100% of them. They used 0% of the lectionaries. Dean Burgon said to use 100% of them. They used only 8% of the total manuscript evidence. Dean Burgon said to use 100% of the manuscript evidence. They used 0% of the ancient versions. They used 0% of the Church Fathers quotations. They only used 426 documents out of 5,575, which is only 7% of the evidence. That is not a Majority of anything. Dean Burgon would not have put his stamp of approval on Price's "*Majority Text*" at all.

# Price's Uncertainty of the Originals

**STATEMENT #53.** (p. 130) "*Finally, there are others who do not regard any one tradition as perfect. . . . No matter what theory a person prefers, **the recovery of the autographic text** is left with some degree of **uncertainty**. This **uncertainty**, no matter how small and insignificant, is a problem. Because it affects one's confidence in **the doctrine of the infallibility and inerrancy of Scripture**.*"

**COMMENT #53.** In the first place, I don't believe that "*the recovery of the autographic text*" is needed. The Words of this text do not need to be "*recovered.*" In fulfillment of God's promise, they have been preserved. They were never lost, so they do not need to be "*recovered.*" These Words are found in the Hebrew, Aramaic, and Greek Words underlying the King James Bible. It is indeed sad that Price has "*uncertainty*" regarding the original Words of the Bible. Price used this word "*uncertainty*" four times on this one page. It sounds like he wants us to join him in his "*uncertainty.*" I don't believe there is any cause for "*uncertainty.*"

---

I have been studying the facts since 1970 when I began studying about this whole subject of the Textus Receptus, the Masoretic Hebrew Text, and the King James Bible. My conclusion is this: I have no "*uncertainty*" as to the preservation of the Old Testament Hebrew and Aramaic Words. I have no "*uncertainty*" as to the preservation of the Greek Words of the New Testament. I believe the original Hebrew, Aramaic and Greek Words are found in the Words underlying our King James Bible. I believe that the King James Bible is an accurate translation of those Hebrew, Aramaic and Greek Words. There is no "*uncertainty*" with me.

# Bible Preservation Not in Translations

` **STATEMENT #54.** (p. 130) Price has a heading at this page: "*Texts May Have Been Preserved in an Authoritative Translation.*" Then he wrote: "*Because of the complexity of the problem of recovering the autographic text from multiple but imperfect witnesses, and because of the uncertainty associated with such a procedure some have resorted to the dogma that God has preserved authoritative translations in various periods of history, and that the English Authorized Version is the perfectly preserved authoritative Word of God for this time.*"

**COMMENT #54.** As I said before, "*recovering the autographic text*" is not our task. It is to believe God promised to preserve His Words and that He has done so. We must discover where He has preserved it and accept it. I believe the King James Bible is the only accurate translation of the preserved Hebrew, Aramaic and Greek Words. When talking about Bible preservation, we should be talking God's preservation of His original Hebrew, Aramaic, and Greek Words, and not about any translation of those Words. Having said that, I believe that the "*English Authorized Version*" (the King James Bible) accurately preserves in the English language the original Hebrew, Aramaic, and Greek Words, but it is impossible to bring over into English all of the nuances of the original Words.

# I Stand For the Traditional Text

**STATEMENT #55.** (p. 130) In Footnote #6, Price wrote: "*Others, such as Edward F. Hills and Donald A. Waite claim to hold the Traditional Text view, but for all practical purposes they defend the King James Only View, see the next note.*"

**COMMENT #55.** Once more, Price utters a most vicious slander, stating that I only "*claim to hold the Traditional Text view*," but in reality he lies about me and says that I "*defend the King James Only View*." As you have been reading this book up to this point, you can see very clearly how much I have despised and refuted the Peter Ruckman "*King James Only*" view. This is Price's greatest deceit. He puts those of us who stand for the inspired, God-breathed, inerrant, preserved original Hebrew, Aramaic, and Greek Words as our foundation as being in the same position as those who stand for the King James Bible as being "*inspired*" and "*God-breathed*" rather than being a "*translation*" only. Price should be ashamed of himself in putting me in this position. Where are his quotations that I hold to the "*King James Only*" viewpoint?

> This King James Only term is a smear term for Ruckmanites. The position of Peter Ruckman is not my position at all and Price knows it, but wants his readers to think that it is.

# Price Puts Me With Peter Ruckman

**STATEMENT #56.** (p. 130) Price makes a further comment in his Footnote #7. After he mentions the name of "*Peter Ruckman*," he mentions "*D. A. Waite, Defending the King James Bible, Collingswood, NJ, The Bible For Today, 1992.*" He then says: "*Some of these authors claim to accept the authority of the Hebrew and Greek texts, but their actual work ends up supporting the English words of the A.V. in every instance. Apart from a few corrections that Hills would admit in marginal notes, nowhere do the others actually propose a correction of the Authorized Version Text. Thus, they virtually accept the English Words as authoritative. Peter Ruckman goes so far as to declare that "the English words of the Authorized Version correct the Greek and Hebrew texts.*"

**COMMENT #56.** This is a libel on the part of James Price. I assume he has read my book, *Defending the King James Bible*, and that he therefore knows better. He believes that I only "*claim*" to "*accept the authority of the Hebrew and Greek texts*," but he doesn't believe it. Where are his quotations from any of my books or messages where I do not "*accept*" this "*authority*"? By saying that "*Peter Ruckman goes so far as to declare that the English words of the Authorized Version correct the Greek and Hebrew texts*," readers might rightly assume that Price is implying that I also hold this heresy that Ruckman holds. This is a serious attack by Price based on deception, lies, and falsehood.

# Price Repeats Two of His Errors

**STATEMENT #57.** (p. 131) "*This view of preservation results in several faulty inferences* [that is, the view that the Bible was preserved through translations]. *First of all, those who hold this view imply that the omniscient, omnipotent God was unable to preserve the original Hebrew and Greek words, He inspired the prophets and apostles to write; consequently, He had to improvise by providentially preserving His word through translations.*"

> **COMMENT #57.** Price shows his utter heresy regarding the important doctrine of the Bible's "*inspiration*." He wrote: "*He inspired the prophets and apostles to write.*" Where is his authority for this? There is none. The "*prophets and apostles*" were "*moved*" or "*borne along*" by the Holy Spirit (2 Peter 1:21), but were never God-breathed or "*inspired.*"

This is a heresy that is all too often repeated. 2 Timothy 3:16's first few words are "*all scripture is given by inspiration of God . . .*" It is the "*Scripture*" (GRAPHE) or "*words*" that were "*given by inspiration of God*" (God-breathed) not the men. Apparently James Price does not know what inspiration means. That is one of the first things you learn in a systematic theology class. It is absolutely heretical to say that God "*inspired*" or "*breathed out*" the prophets and apostles.

A second error of Price's analysis in the above quotation relates to "*preserving His word through translations*." While accurate translations from the preserved original Hebrew, Aramaic, and Greek Words (like the King James Bible) "*preserve*" (with a small "p") God's Words in the language in question (such as in English for the KJB), the ultimate "*Preservation*" (with a capital "P") rests with the Preserved Hebrew, Aramaic, and Greek Words rather than any translation.

# Translations Not Same As Originals

**STATEMENT #58.** (p. 131) "*God's providential supervision of translators is not essentially different from God's sovereign supervision of the prophets and apostles in the first place. So it is essentially the same as the original inspiration.*"

**COMMENT #58.** God's "*providential supervision of translators*" is completely distinct from His "*sovereign supervision of the prophets and apostles*." The "*prophets and apostles*" were "*moved by the Holy Ghost*" (2 Peter 1:21b). No such promise was made to any "*translators*" in all the world. It is false and even heretical to say that "*translations*" are "*essentially the same as the original inspiration*." This is sometimes referred to as "derivative inspiration" and is a false doctrine that cannot be proved either from the Bible or from logic. God did not "*breathe out*" or "*inspire*" English words, Spanish words, German words, Russian words, Japanese words, Chinese words, or words in any other language other than Hebrew, Aramaic and Greek. Derivative "*inspiration*" is false and it should not be held to. It is a deceptive and a confusing term.

# Apostles & Prophets Not "Inspired"

**STATEMENT #59.** (p. 132) Price wrote: "*The view also implies that the original Hebrew and Greek words God inspired the apostles and prophets to write can be perfectly transferred to another language (like English) without* *any loss of precision.*"

**COMMENT #59.** Once again, Price twists the term "*inspiration*" when he uses the phrase, "*the original Hebrew and Greek words God inspired the apostles and prophets to write.*" The word, "*inspired*" comes from the Greek word, THEOPNEUSTOS (2 Timothy 3:16). It means literally "*God-breathed.*" This would not make sense to say, "*God GOD-BREATHED (inspired) the apostles and prophets to write.*" God "*breathed-out*" the Words. This is what "*inspiration*" means. Though a translation can be accurate, it can never be made " *without any loss of precision*" when compared to the *preserved original Hebrew, Aramaic, and Greek Words.*

# Price's Errors of the Hebrew O.T.

**STATEMENT #60.** (p. 133) Price's heading here is: "*The Hebrew Text was Preserved in Ancient Hebrew Bibles.*" He wrote: "*Thus the Hebrew autographs and copies of these early books were written in the Phoenician script. The Phoenician alphabet consisted of consonants only. There were no characters for vowels.*"

**COMMENT #60.** Price is in error once again. It is false to say that "*the Hebrew autographs and copies of these early books were written in the Phoenician script.*" How can he prove this? The Hebrew autographs were written in Hebrew. The Hebrew script does indeed have vowels. Dr. Thomas Strouse has written several articles about the Hebrew vowels. He has shown conclusively that the vowels of the Hebrew text were from the very beginning and were in the original Hebrew text. *Scholarly Myths Perpetuated on Rejecting the Masoretic Text of the Old Testament.* (**BFT** #3197). Dr. Strouse takes this matter up in Myths #2 and #4 in this paper. As Moses wrote the first five books of the Bible, he put the Hebrew vowels within them. In addition, Dr. Strouse shows the necessity for Hebrew vowel points from the beginning in his article entitled *Luke 16:17--One Tittle* (**BFT** #3387). Where is Price's proof that the "*early books*" of the Old Testament were written in the "*Phoenician script*" with "*consonants only*"?

**STATEMENT #61.** (p. 133) "*Some time after the return from Babylonian captivity the scribes began to transliterate the ancient copies of Hebrew scripture into the Aramaic script.*"

**COMMENT #61.** Price wrote that scribes began to "*transliterate the ancient copies of Hebrew scripture into the Aramaic script.*" Where does Price get this error? The original Bible was written in Hebrew with all of its consonants and vowels present, not in "*Babylonian.*" No documentation is given, only his own statement. This is, no doubt, his attempt to remove the vowels from the Hebrew text until a much later time. I deny this emphatically.  Where is his documentary proof?  Where are his preserved Old Testament "*Phoenician*" manuscripts?

**STATEMENT #62.**  (p. 134) Price has a chart Table 7.1 and Table 7.2 showing the "*Phoenician Script*" and the "*Hebrew and Phoenician Scripts*" side by side.

**COMMENT #62.**  I don't know what Price is attempting to prove by the comparisons of these letters.  It does not prove that the Hebrew script was not used from the very first.  Nor does it prove that the Phoenician script was used in the "*early copies*" of our Old Testament.  It is pure speculation on his part.  It is an "*evolutionary*" framework that he has developed with as little proof as "*evolution*" itself.

# False Date of the Septuagint (LXX)

**STATEMENT #63.**  (p. 134)  "*The Jews who settled in Alexandria, Egypt, adopted the Greek language and culture of that area. Near the middle of the 3rd Century B.C., the Hebrew Scriptures were translated into Greek for use in the synagogues and schools. Known as the Septuagint, this translation was made from the Hebrew text tradition current in that area, and it is the primary witness to this text tradition.*"

**COMMENT #63.**  Price has adopted the false position that "*the Septuagint*" was translated from the Hebrew in "*3rd Century B.C.*"  Though there are a few books that were produced in Greek B.C., no one anywhere in the world has produced the entire Old Testament from Genesis through Malachi that was B.C. If Price can produce such a volume, I will believe him.  Otherwise, it is pure speculation of the worst sort.  The earliest date of the Septuagint is the one produced by Origen in his *Hexapla* in the 200's A.D.  A further error is made when Price said that the "*Septuagint*" is the "*primary witness*" of this "*Hebrew text tradition.*"  On the contrary, the Hebrew Words themselves are always the "*primary witness*" to the "*Hebrew text*" rather than some A.D. Greek translation called the "*Septuagint.*"

# Price Denies Original Hebrew Vowels

**STATEMENT #64.**  (pp. 136-137)  "*Starting about the 5th Century A.D. the Jews began to address the preservation of the Traditional oral pronunciation of the text in public reading. By this time, the consonantal text was so sacred that no new characters could be invented and added to the text to represent the vowels. Instead, various methods were tried for indicating* *the vowels by means of simple diacritical marks above or below the consonants."*

**COMMENT #64.** Price is saying that *"about the 5ᵗʰ Century A.D."* the Hebrew *"vowels"* came into being. This means that he believes there were no *vowels* in the Hebrew Words of the Bible until that time, but only Hebrew consonants. Though this is the current position, it is seriously false. Dr. Thomas Strouse, the Academic Dean of the Emmanuel Baptist Theological Seminary, has written an excellent and convincing article on the originality of the *"vowels."* He proves that the Hebrew vowels had to have been present in the autographic Hebrew Words when Moses penned the first five books of the Bible. They must have been present in every other Old Testament Hebrew book as well. They had to be present in order to make clear the exact Hebrew Words used in the Bible. The reason for this is that the same Hebrew consonants without the *"vowels"* can mean many different words. In this event, there could be no **verbal** plenary inspiration of the Old Testament. That would be a serious failure in the theological area of Bibliology.

**STATEMENT #65.** (p. 136) In footnote 17, Price wrote: *"Originally the Hebrew Scriptures were written only in consonants. The vowels and accent marks were added by the Masoretes in about the 9ᵗʰ Century A.D."*

---

**COMMENT #65.** Price had formerly said that in the *"5ᵗʰ Century"* the vowel marking came in. Now he is saying that it was *"about the 9ᵗʰ Century A.D."* when the Hebrew *"vowels"* entered the Old Testament. If this were true (and it is not), it would mean that for about 2,000 years, no one on earth would have really known what the actual Words of the Old Testament were because there were no vowels to accurately identify the Words. This would be a serious error, though this is what I was taught at Dallas Theological Seminary. As I said previously, Dr. Thomas Strouse has documented a powerful case to prove that the vowels were with the consonants in the original Hebrew Words that Moses and all of the Old Testament writers wrote. This is found in his paper entitled *Scholarly Myths Perpetuated on Rejecting the Masoretic Text of the Old Testament* (BFT #3197). He deals with this in Myths #2 & 4. In addition, Dr. Strouse shows the necessity for Hebrew vowel points from the beginning in his article entitled *Luke 16:17--One Tittle* (BFT #3387).

---

# Septuagint (LXX) A.D. Recensions

**STATEMENT #66.** (p. 139-140) Under the heading, *"The Greek Text Was Preserved in Ancient Greek Bibles,"* Price quoted Jerome (347-420 A.D.) concerning restorations or recensions of the Greek Old Testament or

Septuagint: *"Jerome, who wrote about A.D. 400, mentioned three recensions that were current in his day."*

**COMMENT #66.** Price is now speaking of the Greek translation of the Old Testament called the Septuagint. It was made in A.D., not in B.C. as Price believes. It evidently had various editions that Jerome mentioned.

# Very Few Alexandrian Greek MSS

**STATEMENT #67.** (p. 140) Price is speaking on a heading called *"The Alexandrian Tradition*." He wrote of this Alexandrian text: *"The introduction of translations and the rise of persecution account for the relatively few ancient manuscript witnesses in this tradition in existence today."*

**COMMENT #67.** I agree with Price when he talked about the *"relatively few ancient manuscript witnesses to this tradition in existence today."* In saying this, he is talking about the *"**Alexandrian tradition**"* of the Gnostic Vatican and Sinai manuscripts. The *"fewness"* is indicative of the early church's disdain for them due to their heretical Gnostic doctrines. The early church refused to copy them, leaving only Vatican and Sinai plus about forty-three other manuscripts. Yet, upon these forty-five or so inferior Gnostic heretical *"manuscripts"* (less than 1% of the manuscript evidence), the Roman Catholic leaders, the liberal Protestant leaders, the new Evangelical leaders, and altogether too many Fundamentalist leaders agree with this error. In contrast, our New Testament should be founded upon the some 5,210 superior manuscripts (over 99% of the manuscript evidence) which form the basis of our King James Bible.

This manuscript evidence can be found in a book by Dr. Jack Mormon called *Forever Settled* **(BFT #1428 @ $20.00 + $5.00 S&H)**. Dr. Moorman takes the data from the 1967 documentation by Kurt Aland of Munster, Germany. Aland said as of that date, there were 5,255 manuscripts that have been preserved. Though there have been discovered around 300 more manuscripts since then, it is assumed that the breakdown and percentages would remain the same.

# Very Few Western Greek MSS

**STATEMENT #68.** (pp. 141-142) When talking about *"The Western Tradition,"* Price said: *"Because most Christians in the West did not continue to use Greek, and because Latin translations became available, the demand for Greek Bibles diminished in those areas. This accounts for the relatively few Greek manuscripts in this tradition in existence today ."*

**COMMENT #68.** Price is correct about the "*relatively few Greek manuscripts in this tradition in existence today.*" The same can be said of the so-called "*Caesarean Tradition*" that Price talks about in a similar section. The bottom line is that the so-called Critical Text of the New Testament manuscripts number about 45. This resembles a miniature dwarf when compared to the more than 5,210 manuscripts of the great giant Traditional Received Text.

# No Lucian Recension

**STATEMENT #69.** (p. 143) In footnote #38, Price wrote: "*Scholars who prefer the priority of the Byzantine Text deny a Lucian Recension or one like it. They prefer to assume that the Byzantine Tradition derives directly from autographic text.*"

**COMMENT #69.** Why shouldn't we "*deny a Lucian recension*"? There is no proof of a "*Lucian recension.*" This is what Professor Hort and Bishop Westcott have tried to allege. Dean John W. Burgon made it clear that there is not any proof of any kind that (1) the leaders of all Christendom came together in Lucian's time or at either 150 A.D. or 250 A.D.; (2) brought their manuscripts to the meetings; (3) threw out all the critical manuscripts and; (4) kept only the Traditional Text manuscripts. Price is saying that this "*recension*" or revision happened. He believes that this is how the Traditional Text manuscripts have a predominance over the Critical Text manuscripts. The fact of the matter is that if something of that historical proportion occurred where all the religious leaders of that day got together to make a recension, it would have been recorded in history somewhere. Yet it appears nowhere in history. This is a totally false fairy tale that was cleverly concocted by Professor Hort to try to advance his lies. Price, along with many others, has bought into the falsehood.

# Price's Wrong Syriac Version

**STATEMENT #70.** (p. 143) Price wrote about the Syriac version in footnote #39 as follows: "*This translation is limited to the Harklean Syriac version. Other Syrian versions seem to support the Western Tradition.*"

**COMMENT #70.** Actually, the "*Syriac version*" mentioned here is not the "*Harklean*" but is the Syriac Peshitta which is the earliest translation of the "*Syriac.*" Though Critical Text people deny its date, it was actually dated about 150 A.D. and favors the Traditional Received Text in most places. It is wrong to say that the earliest "*Syriac*" was the "*Harklean*" which is a Critical Text.

# The "Byzantine" Traditional Text

**STATEMENT #71.** (p. 145) Price is writing about "*The Byzantine Tradition.*" He said: "*Since this form of the text survived in the Greek-speaking churches, no translations were made of this later form of the text—there was no need. Many textual authorities regard this Byzantine Text to be late and of secondary importance.*"

**COMMENT #71.** Though Dean Burgon never used the name of this text, "*The Byzantine Tradition,*" in my opinion, it is a name for the Traditional Received Text. There are two errors in Price's words that "*no translations were made of this later form of the text.*" (1) Error #1 is that many translations were made of this Traditional Received Text and are still being made. (2) Error #2 is that the Traditional Received Text is not a "*later form of the text.*" On the contrary, it is the original text of the New Testament that came from the hands of the writers.

Price's words, "*this Byzantine Text to be late and of secondary importance*" are also false. Again, there are two major errors in these words: (1) The so-called "*Byzantine Text*" is not "*late.*" It was the original text of the New Testament with over 99% of the manuscripts (5,210) behind it. (2) This text is not "*of secondary importance.*" Rather, it is of major and primary importance. It is the Gnostic Critical Text with only 1% of the manuscripts (45) that is of "*secondary importance.*"

**STATEMENT #72.** p. 145 "*On the other hand, other textual scholars regard this text tradition to be the most authoritative.*"

**COMMENT #72.** I certainly agree with this statement by Price. The Byzantine Traditional Received Text is "*the most authoritative.*"

# No Genealogy in Greek MSS

**STATEMENT #73.** (p. 146) Price has a figure 7.2 chart here that is labeled "*Genealogy of the Greek New Testament.*" It is a simplified diagram that seeks to prove a genealogical relationship between various text traditions.

**COMMENT #73.** There is no such thing as a "*genealogical*" relationship in Greek New Testament manuscripts. Price has adopted the genealogical fallacy put forth first by Professor Hort in his 1881 *Introduction* to the Westcott and Hort Greek text. Hort postulated, without a shred of evidence, that there were various textual families. Price begins with the "*Autographic Text*" calls them (1) "*Egyptian*" (Alexandrian); (2)

*"Western,"* (3) *"Caesarean,"* and (4) *"Antiochan"* (*Byzantine, Traditional, Received*).  By this chart, Price is showing that he believes in textual *"families."*

> The only problem with this falsehood is that there is no proof of it whatsoever.  As Dean Burgon has stated, there is only one textual tradition, not four.  He illustrated it by saying that it is like going into a cemetery with unmarked graves.  You cannot prove that any of the people buried in the cemetery are related to each other.  This is the case with the Greek New Testament.  Each manuscript is a lone and independent document.  Here's what he wrote:
>
> *"The living inhabitants of a village, congregated in the churchyard where the bodies of their forgotten progenitors for 1000 years repose without memorials of any kind,* [In other words, there are no gravestones in this cemetery.]*—is a faint image of the relation which subsists between extant copies of the Gospels and the sources from which they were derived."* [Dean John W. Burgon, *Revision Revised*, p. 256].

## Price's Uncertainty

**STATEMENT #74.** (p. 151) Price's heading is *"The Manuscripts are Variously Distributed"*    He wrote: *"Those who attempt to evade the* **uncertainty** *inherent in the text do so by overly simplifying the solution and by holding to dogmatic suppositions.  Such approaches exceed what God has clearly revealed in His Word."*

> **COMMENT #74.** Do you get the idea that Price has a lot of *"uncertainty"*?  I have no *"uncertainty."*  Price has *"uncertainty."*  He does not know the exact Words of the Bible.  If he has such *"uncertainty,"* how can he preach?  How can he teach?  I have the certainty that I have the original and preserved Hebrew, Aramaic and Greek Words which underlie the King James Bible.  I am certain that the King James Bible is the only accurate translation from the preserved original Hebrew, Aramaic and Greek Words.  I am trying to instill this certainty into my readers of this book, and the many other books that I have published.  Price is to be pitied for having so much *"uncertainty."*

## Preservation Not in Translations

**STATEMENT #75.** (p. 153) Price's Chapter 8 is entitled *"The Biblical Text was **Preserved in Ancient Translations**."*

**COMMENT #75.** This title is completely misleading and false. The means that God used in the preservation of His Words was not "*Ancient Translations*" or any other "*translations*." His means was the verbal, plenary preservation of the original Hebrew, Aramaic, and Greek Words. How can you get verbal, plenary preservation by "*translations*" which vary the Words of the Bible in many different ways?

# Witness of Ancient Versions to TR

**STATEMENT #76.** (p. 153) "*However, Textus Receptus and KJV-only advocates have misinterpreted Burgon to mean that the witness of the ancient versions consistently support the Traditional Text against the 'Alexandria' text which they regard as corrupt and heretical.*"

**COMMENT #76.** Here again, Price has made the false representation that the "*Textus Receptus and KJV- only advocates*" are to be identified as one group. Once again, I totally repudiate being any part of the Peter Ruckman followers who identify themselves as "*KJV-only*." Their errors abound and I do not share any of them. If Price were honest, he would write a separate book against the Ruckmanite "*KJV-only*" people and a separate book on those of us who are based on the "*Textus Receptus*" for the New Testament and the Hebrew and Aramaic Words underlying the King James Bible for the Old Testament.

I have not "*misinterpreted Burgon*" as Price charges. I have never stated in any of my books or messages that the "*ancient versions consistently support the Traditional Text.*" Sometimes they support the "*Traditional Text*" and sometimes they do not. In the case of Mark 16:9-20, the last twelve verses of Mark. there are ten "*ancient versions*" that follow the "*Traditional Text*" and contain these verses. Price is correct when he mentions the "*'Alexandria' text which they regard as corrupt and heretical.*" The Gnostic "*Alexandria text*" used by the Vatican and Sinai manuscripts and their forty-three followers indeed are "*corrupt and heretical.*"

# The False "Letter of Aristeas"

**STATEMENT #77.** (p. 156) Price made reference on the previous page to the "*legendary account given in the Letter of Aristeas*" about the origin of the Septuagint. He then wrote: "*The account is clearly a legend, but it reflects an actual historic event.*"

**COMMENT #77.** Does this statement: "*The account is clearly a legend, but it reflects an actual historic event*" make sense? How

> can a "*legend*" reflect an "*actual historic event*"? Price, himself, admits it is just a "*legend*." The *Legend of Sleepy Hollow* is not true. It is merely a story. There is no truth in legends they are fairy tales.

# The Lie of a B.C. Septuagint (LXX)

**STATEMENT #78.** (p. 156) *"For example, the quality of the translation of Daniel was so poor that many later Greek Bibles replaced the LXX Daniel with the translation of Theodotian. However, the whole Old Testament was completed in the middle of the second Century B.C. "*

**COMMENT #78.** It is false for Price to say that "*the whole Old Testament was completed in the middle of the second Century B.C.*" Again, I ask Price to prove that there was an entire Greek translation of the Old Testament from Genesis to Malachi B.C. All he has to do is (1) to get it in his possession (2) invite some impartial observers to examine it closely (3) make an affidavit before a notary public (4) send me a copy, and I will believe it. Failing of that, I will not believe it! Since I know for a positive fact that Price or any others who believe this lie cannot produce such a B.C. "*Septuagint*," they should stop repeating this fairy tale as if it were true. "*Lie not one to another, seeing that ye have put off the old man with his deeds*" (Colossians 3:9).

**STATEMENT #79.** (p. 156) ". . . *many of the New Testament quotations of the Old Testament were taken from the LXX*. Likewise, manuscripts of *portions of the LXX were found among the Dead Sea Scrolls* from the first century B.C. and earlier, substantiating an early pre-Christian date for the LXX."

**COMMENT #79.** Price is quoting about Philo (c. 10 B.C. to A.D.50) and Josephus (A.D. 37-100). When he said: "*many of the New Testament quotations of the Old Testament were taken from the LXX*," it is false. They were taken from the Hebrew Words and modified as the Lord Jesus Christ instructed God the Holy Spirit for His own emphasis for the New Testament. How would it be possible to quote from a document that was not even in existence until the 200's A.D.? As far as Price's statement that "*New Testament quotations of the Old Testament were taken from the LXX*, there indeed may have been "*portions*" of the Old Testament in Greek, but not the entire Genesis through Malachi.

**STATEMENT #80.** (p. 157) In footnote #9, quoting Peter Ruckman, Price wrote: "*But if a thousand pieces of papyrus were recovered with Old Testament Greek on them written before 100 B.C. nothing could bolster the* *sagging testimony of the LXX.*"

**COMMENT #80.** This argument is enlightening. We cannot be satisfied with simply a few "*pieces of papyrus*" here and there. Price must have an entire B.C. Old Testament in the Greek language before he can prove it to be written B.C. Since he cannot do this, why doesn't he just keep quiet about it? Should we deal with facts, or just opinions?

# Price Praises Apostate Origen

**STATEMENT #81.** (p. 158) "*Between A.D. 230 and 240, Origen (A.D. 155-254) a brilliant theologian in Alexandria, undertook to resolve the variations between the Hebrew text and the differing Greek versions existing in his day. . . . The fifth* [column] *contained his own revision of the LXX.*"

**COMMENT #81.** As to the statement, "*Origen (A.D. 155-254) a brilliant theologian in Alexandria,*" let me tell a few things he believed. I'll let you decide how "*brilliant*" a "*theologian*" he was. I'm quoting from a new book by Dr. H. D. Williams entitled *Origin of the Critical Text* (**BFT #3386 @ $20.00**):

---

# Some of Origen's Apostate Beliefs

1. "*He sided with Arius in his teachings that Jesus was a created being who was not eternally generated.*

2. *He denied a literal Hell.*

3. *He denied a physical resurrection.*

4. *Origen also believed in the preexistence of the human soul.*

5. *He believed in regeneration by baptism* [I am omitting #6 from a list.]

6. *(Not important so not listed)*

7. *He taught transubstantiation.*

8. *He alleged that Satan was paid a ransom by Christ's death, which allowed a 'mystical kiss,' whatever that means.*

9. *He allegorically dismissed the Passover, Jesus' wilderness temptation, and the purging of Herod's temple.*

10. *He accepted the Apocrypha and attributed the 'Shepherd of Hermas' to inspiring his allegorical system.*

11. *He had very little faith in the Scriptures.*

12. *His mental faculties may have also been affected by his self-mutilation, the act of castrating himself.*" (pp. 83-84)

---

I'll let you be the judge of how "*brilliant*" Origen's "*theology*" was. I think he was a leading Gnostic heretic and a theological moron.

As for Price's statement that Origen's fifth column of his Hexapla contained "*his own revision of the LXX*," I don't believe it for a minute. Origen was the author and originator of the Old Testament Greek translation known as the Septuagint. He didn't "*revise*" it, he authored it.

# Origen's 5ᵗʰ Column in His Hexapla

**STATEMENT #82.** (p. 158) Price is speaking of Origen's Hexapla of six columns. He wrote: "*His fifth column contains special marks indicating how he modified the LXX*."

**COMMENT #82.** Price has no proof of this. Where is the so-called "*original LXX*" that Origen was supposed to have revised? In order to have a "*revision*" you have to have something to revise. Where is it? Price can't prove it. He is just guessing. **His teachers and friends have given him this line and he just spouts it in his book, hoping that others might believe it without any questions.**

# Price's False Date of the Peshitta

**STATEMENT #83.** (pp. 161-162) Price wrote: "*At the beginning of the fifth century, the Peshitta*, or the common Syriac version was translated."

**COMMENT #83.** This date is false. Price falsely said that the "*old Syriac*" was dated "*in the middle of the first century A.D.*" Then he falsifies the date of "*the Peshitta*" as being "*At the beginning of fifth century*." On the contrary, "*the Peshitta*" should be dated in the second century (*The Traditional Text*, **BFT #1159**, p. 74) , around 150 A.D. as Dean John W. Burgon and Edward Miller have clearly proven.

# Ruckman & King James-Only Term

**STATEMENT #84.** (p. 162) Speaking about the Peshitta Syriac version, Price said in footnotes #31 and 32, "*Burgon described this version as 'a text so near to the original text as the Peshitta must ever have been. . . . The mention of doctrinal heresy is significant here because the Textus Receptus and the King James-only advocates of the Byzantine Text place a great deal of importance on the alleged heretical views of the Alexandrian Churches. Heresy is one reason they conclude that the non-Byzantine traditions are corrupt and unreliable. But if heresy is a criterion, then they must also reject the Syriac versions in order to be consistent*."

**COMMENT #84.** Here Price again places "*the Textus Receptus and the King James-only advocates*" together in order to smear the "*Textus Receptus*" people like myself with the Peter Ruckmanite "*King*

*James- only*" term. I object! I prefer the Textus Receptus, and I also prefer the King James Bible. The Ruckmanites prefer the King James Bible period. They don't need the "***Textus Receptus***." That's where this "***King James-only***" epithet came from.

> The Ruckman people think that the King James Version English is a special revelation that came directly from God including the italics, so they forget the "***Textus Receptus***." My position is that we need the Hebrew, Aramaic and Greek Words that underlie our King James Bible as well as our King James Bible.

Then Price talks about "***the alleged heretical views of the Alexandrian Churches***." He is down-playing "***heresy***" as if it doesn't exist in his favorite "***Alexandrian***" Texts of the Vatican and the Sinai. He is almost making fun of it. Dr. Jack Moormon, one of our church's missionaries in London, England, has carefully researched these critical Greek texts and specifies over 356 doctrinal passages in these texts where there is doctrinal error. These are listed in his book, *Early Manuscripts, Church Fathers, and the Authorized Version* (BFT #3230 @ $20.00 + $5.00 S&H) on pages119-312. Dr. Moorman identifies over 356 doctrinal passages where the New International Version (NIV), by following their Gnostic-contaminated Critical Texts, has erred from sound doctrine. I detail 158 of these 356 doctrinal passages in Chapter V of my book, *Defending the King James Bible*. I show how heresy is there. I quote from the Vatican ("B") and the Sinai (Aleph) manuscripts. I quote from the versions that use the "B" and "Aleph" (Vatican and Sinai) Alexandria Manuscripts.

# Dr. D. O. Fuller Linked to Ruckman

**STATEMENT #85.** (p. 165)  In footnote #40, Price refers to Dr. David Otis Fuller's book, *Which Bible*. He wrote: "*David Otis Fuller . . . reproduced several chapters from Seventh Day Adventist Benjamin Wilkinson's book, Our Authorized Version Vindicated . . .194-215. Fuller approved Wilkinson's conclusion that ___the Waldensian Version preserved the original text___ through the Old Latin tradition. ___Wilkinson's reconstruction of history is also accepted by Peter Ruckman and his followers. Ruckman includes the old Latin manuscripts in his list of 'good Bibles.'___*"

**COMMENT #84.** There is nothing wrong with believing that "***the Waldensian Version preserved the original text***." It has been shown by Dean Burgon and others that the Waldenses had a Traditional Text New Testament. I list this position in my book, *Defending the King James Bible*, pp. 45-46 (BFT #1594 @ $12.00 + $5.00 S&P). "*The old Latin manuscripts*" are indeed largely in the Traditional Text camp. This has been established by Dean

Burgon and others. It is not the exclusive position of Ruckman as Price seems to imply.

> Once again Price seeks to link Dr. Fuller and other non-Ruckmanites with Peter Ruckman by saying: "*Wilkinson's reconstruction of history is also accepted by Peter Ruckman and his followers.*" It was not a "*reconstruction of history*" but was history itself. While it is true that Dr. Benjamin Wilkinson was a Seventh Day Adventist, he wrote an important book, *Our Authorized Version Vindicated.* Our Bible For Today ministry carries that book in reprint format. It is a good book standing historically for the King James Bible and the underlying Greek texts and it is an excellent volume with many good arguments. Price should answer the arguments that Wilkinson makes rather than just to smear the book by use of his church. His religion is not even brought up in the book. His arguments in the book itself cannot be denied.

# The Old Latin

**STATEMENT #86.** (p. 167)   Price, in speaking of the Old Latin version, stated: "*Most of the manuscripts are incomplete. Therefore, contrary to the claims of the KJV-Only advocates, the old Latin does not validate the Traditional Text (TR).*"

**COMMENT #86.**   Price is in error, despite his Table 8.2 which attempts to discredit "*the Old Latin*" as a largely Traditional Text document.

> Dean John W. Burgon says the old Latin in many places is close to the Textus Receptus. It has many words and verses close to our Textus Receptus.

# Preservation Not in Church Fathers

**STATEMENT #87.** (p. 175)   Price entitles Chapter 9 "*Biblical Text was Preserved in Patristic Quotations*"

**COMMENT #87.**   The "*Patristic quotations*" or allusions were from the Church Fathers. Once again, Price has the wrong idea of what "*preserved*" means. For him, he does not define it, as I do, to mean verbal plenary preservation. No Church father can "*preserve*" the Words of God exactly, but Price doesn't mind that, because for his "*preservation*," he needs only the "*ideas, thoughts, concepts, and teachings*" but not the **Words**.

# The Use of Church Fathers

**STATEMENT #88.** (p. 175) He quoted Dean Burgon on this: *"John W. Burgon regarded the testimony of an early Christian writer commonly referred to as a __Church father__ to be superior to that of any single ancient manuscript. He declared, 'The testimony of any first rate father, where it can be had must be held to outweigh the solitary testimony of any single Codex which can be named.' Again he asserted: 'Individually, therefore, a father's evidence, when it can certainly be obtained . . . is considerably greater than that of any single known Codex.'"*

**COMMENT #88.** The *__Church Fathers__* did sometimes quote from the Traditional Text and sometimes from the other text. What Dean Burgon is saying is that if you have a specific Church father, you know what kind of Bible he had in his hand when he quoted or alluded to a verse. We know of him. We know when he lived and when he died. We know some of the books, articles, and letters he authored. If an early Church father quotes a Traditional manuscript word or phrase that is not in the Critical Text, it proves that he had a copy of a Traditional manuscript in his hands at that early date. It also shows that the Traditional Text is early, not late. The Critical Text people say that you can't use these Church Fathers, and this is false. Dean Burgon has gathered together some 186,000 quotations from the early Church Fathers. He shows from these, without any shadow of doubt, the usefulness of quotations from Church Fathers.

The followers of the Critical Text say that the Traditional Text was not in existence during the times of the Church Fathers. Dean Burgon fixed that by taking a sampling of 76 Church Fathers' Bible quotations or allusions to see how many either alluded to or quoted exactly from the Traditional Text. That is exactly what he did.

> Dean Burgon and his assistants looked at the writings of these 76 early Church Fathers' writings. He found that out of those Church Fathers who died in 400 A.D. or before, there was a majority ratio of 3 to 2 quotations or allusions to the Traditional Text as opposed to the Critical Text. This is 60% versus 40%. This is found in Dean Burgon's book, *The Traditional Text* (BFT #1159, pp. 99 and following).

It shows that the Bible they had in their hands was the Traditional Text that underlies our King James Bible. A 60% to 40% majority of Church Fathers quotations or allusions was from the Traditional Textus Receptus that underlies our King James Bible. Does that not prove Price and his followers are wrong in their falsehoods in saying that our Textus Receptus was not in existence during Apostolic times. They are dead wrong and this is a lie. Dr.

Jack Moorman also made a study of the Church Fathers. He found in his study that the Church Fathers who died A.D. 400 or before used Traditional Textus Receptus readings that underlie our King James Bible in a majority of 70% to 30%. Seventy percent of the quotations were Traditional Textus Receptus quotations and 30% were from the Critical Text.

# Preservation Is Not O.T. Quotes

**STATEMENT #89.** (p. 177) Price has this heading: "*Quotations of the Old Testament Preserved the Text.*"

**COMMENT #89.** Mere "*Quotations of the Old Testament*" do not "*Preserve the Text.*" It must be the Words themselves in Hebrew or Greek in manuscript form. "*Quotations*" can be loose and not accurate in many cases. It illustrates Price's woefully inaccurate understanding of what Bible "*preservation*" really means. Bible "preservation" does not rest in "*quotations*" only, but in the very Hebrew, Aramaic, and Greek Words. For him, it means only the loose "*thoughts, ideas, concepts, or teachings*" rather than Words.

# Value of Church Fathers & the TR

**STATEMENT #90.** (p. 178) Price refers to Table 9.1, "*Distribution of Fathers by Date.*" He wrote: "*Unfortunately most of these witnesses are incomplete, making the witness to the whole text unavailable. Burgon provided a survey of the witnesses of the fathers to the Gospels and a survey of the early Church Fathers that seemed to favor the Traditional Text in the gospels .*"

**COMMENT #90.** Some Fundamentalist writers today, who favor the Critical Text, have said that there is no trace of the Traditional Received Text prior to the 6th Century. This is entirely false. Dean Burgon and his staff examined 76 Church Fathers who died in 400 A.D. or before, to see if there were a Traditional Text or Textus Receptus type of text in the writings and quotations of these early Church Fathers.

> The Church Fathers were leaders of the churches in the early days of the church age. In the course of their debating and writing one to another in those early years, 400 A.D. or before, they quoted or alluded to New Testament verses in the Bible. Those allusions or quotations of the early Church Fathers are important to determine what Greek text they had in their hands in their day.

This is one of the things that modern textual critics (like Price) are differing with and are not willing to look into. These quotes show that the Bible they had in their hands, in many cases, used the Traditional Received kind of manuscript. This also proves that our Textus Receptus was early and not late.

> Dean Burgon took a total of 76 early Church Fathers, and from their writings determined the percentage that these Church Fathers quoted from the Traditional Text and the Critical Text. He found 60% of the Church Fathers quotations were from the Textus Receptus or Traditional Text and only 40% were from the Critical Text. Dr. Jack Moorman also made a study. He found 70% of the church father's quotations were from the Traditional Text and only 30% were from the Critical Text.

**STATEMENT #91.** (p. 180) Price's conclusion of the discussion of the Church Fathers was: "*Conclusion:  the witness of the quotations is incomplete and secondary*."

**COMMENT #91.** When Price stated that "*the witness of the quotations is incomplete and secondary*," he is dead wrong, as he has been in many other things. The "*witness of the quotations*" is not "*secondary*," it is "*primary*". Here is the reason I say this. The Critical Text propaganda-line is that their favorite fourth century Gnostic heretical Vatican and Sinai manuscripts were tantamount to the originals themselves. The Traditional Received Words underlying the King James Bible are despised by them. One of the things these dishonest Critical Text charlatans claim is that there were no Traditional Received Words in existence until very late–the 6th Century or later. The quotations or allusions by the Church Fathers puts the lie to this because the fathers are dated. Dean Burgon and his staff showed of the 76 Church Fathers examined that the Traditional Received Words were not only there, they were in the majority of the citations. And not only a simple majority, but in the ratio of 3 to 2 or 60% to 40%. (See his *Traditional Text*, pp. 99 ff. in **BFT #1159**). Dr. Jack Moorman did a similar study and found the ratio to be 70% to 30% in favor of the Traditional Received Text (see *Early Manuscripts, Church Fathers, and the Authorized Version* **BFT #3230**). I don't know when this ignorance on the part of the Critical Text-only people, both saved and lost, will cease.

In the mind of Price and many others, why are the Church Fathers "*secondary*"? I believe one of the reasons is that it proves them to be in serious error. If you are **really** trying to find out the situation as to what Bibles these Church Fathers had in their hands in 100 A.D., in 200 A.D., in 300 A.D., or in 400 A.D., then these 186,000 quotations or allusions to their Bibles in the hands of these Church Fathers are extremely important. These quotes are not "*secondary*" they are "*primary*." No Greek manuscript has a date, but these Church Fathers have dates, as to when they lived. This proves that the Church Fathers had in their hands, without any doubt whatsoever, many of the original

Traditional Received Words.

# Gnostic Heretical "Alexandrian Text"

**STATEMENT #92.** (p. 181) Price's Chapter 10 is entitled: "*Some Recognize the Alexandrian Text as the Preserved Text*"

**COMMENT #92.** The "*Alexandrian Text*" is found in the Vatican and Sinai manuscripts and a few of their followers. It was doctored by the Gnostic heretics whose false religion was located in Alexandria, Egypt. It is also called the Critical Text. The Vatican and Sinai manuscripts differ from the Traditional Received Words underlying the King James Bible in over 8,000 places. See *8,000 Differences Between the Critical Text and the Traditional Text* by Dr. Jack Moorman **(BFT #3084 for a gift of $20.00 + $5.00 S&H)**]. This text has over 356 doctrinal passages that are in error. See *Early MSS, Church Fathers, & the Authorized Version* by Dr. Jack Moorman **(BFT #3230 for a gift of $20.00 + $5.00 S&H.)**].

# The Traditional Received Text

**STATEMENT #93.** (p. 181) Price wrote: "*The Traditional Text, or Textus Receptus (the text of the Reformation) is regarded as the authoritative text by some Protestants.*"

**COMMENT #93.** That is correct. It is "*regarded as the authoritative text*" by me, though I am not a "*Protestant*," but an independent Baptist. It is not only "*the text of the Reformation*," but I believe that the form of the "*Traditional Received Text*" that underlies the King James Bible is the preserved Hebrew, Aramaic, and Greek Words of the original New Testament.

**STATEMENT #94.** (p. 181) "*The Traditional Text is sometimes equated with the Byzantine Text, but that assumption is erroneous.*"

> **COMMENT #94.** I don't believe it is erroneous. Though Dean John W. Burgon never used the term, "*Byzantine Text*," it is just another name for what he termed the "*Traditional Text*." Price, and many others are wrong in these definitions.

# Errors of So-Called "Majority Text"

**STATEMENT #95.** (p. 181) "*The Byzantine Tradition is recognized as the authoritative text by the Greek Orthodox Church, and also by some among the Protestant groups. This text tradition is also known as the Majority Text because it is represented by the majority of existing manuscripts. The Majority Text view is the topic of Chapter 11.*"

**COMMENT #95.** The "*Byzantine Tradition*" is the same as what Dean Burgon referred to as the "*Traditional Text*." It has been commandeered by a certain group of people. The attempt has been to separate the Traditional Received Text from the co-called "*Byzantine Tradition*."

As for the so-called "*Majority Text*," that Price espouses, it is ridiculous to call it a "majority" of anything. There are two "*Majority Texts*" that compete with one another in many areas. The first one to come out in the 1980's was by Zane Hodges and Arthur Farstad of Dallas Theological Seminary (my own school).

> The "*Majority Text*" differs from the Traditional Received Text in 1,500 to 1,800 places. It was based on Von Sodden's textual notes. Von Sodden had only about 414 manuscripts. Even if every one of Von Sodden's notes were accepted, how is this a "*majority*" of anything? Even in 1967, Kurt Aland had 5,255 Greek manuscripts. There are now 300 or 400 more since then. But how dare these "*Majority Text*" fanatics say that these 414 are a "*majority*" of 5,355! For a complete critique of this "*Majority Text*" you should get *Hodges and Farstad's Majority Text Refuted* (BFT #1617 @ $16.00 + $5.00 S&H). It is by Dr. Jack Moorman.

# Westcott & Hort, an Alexandrian Text

**STATEMENT #96.** (p. 181) "*Advocates of the Traditional Text and the Byzantine Text erroneously assume that Westcott and Hort recognized the Alexandrian Tradition as the authoritative text. In fact, this assumption is an over-simplification of the situation. Westcott and Hort developed a theory of textual criticism based on the method used by classical philologists.*"

**COMMENT #96.** It is total falsehood to say people "*erroneously assume that Westcott and Hort recognized the Alexandrian Tradition as the authoritative text*." They most certainly did! The two leading manuscripts of this "*Alexandrian Tradition*" were the Vatican ("B") and the Sinai (Aleph). I concur with Dean John W. Burgon's statements on this matter. Let me quote two sections of Dean Burgon's *Revision Revised* as to "*Westcott and Hort's*" belief in the "*supremacy*" of the Vatican and Sinai manuscripts, especially that of the Vatican ("B.")

"*All this is followed, of course, by the weak fable of the 'Neutral' Text, and of the absolute supremacy of Codex B--which is "stated in Dr. Hort's own words:"--viz. "B very far exceeds all other documents in neutrality of text, being in fact always, or nearly always, neutral.*" (*The Revision Revised*, p. 396).

*XLVI. And thus, by an unscrupulous use of the process of Reiteration, accompanied by a boundless exercise of the imaginative faculty, we have reached the goal to which all that went before has been steadily tending : viz. the absolute supremacy of codices B and Aleph above all other codices,–and, when they differ, then of codex B*. (*The Revision Revised*, p. 304)

If the Sinai manuscript ("Aleph") manuscript did not agree with the "B" or Vatican Manuscript "*Westcott and Hort*" threw out the "Aleph" Manuscript and used some other manuscript that went along with their "B" Manuscript.

# Westcott & Hort & the Vatican MS

**STATEMENT #97.** (pp. 181-182) "*It is true that they regarded the Alexandrian Tradition as more reliable than the others, but they did weigh the evidence of the other text traditions, and accepted the witness of the other traditions when the weight of evidence overruled the Alexandrian Tradition.*"

**COMMENT #97.** This is absolutely false. Westcott and Hort worshipped this Gnostic "**Vatican**" ("B") and Sinai (Aleph) manu-scripts. I believe Price is in serious error when he says that Westcott and Hort "*did weigh the evidence.*" It is an equal error to say that these two men "*accepted the witness of the other traditions.*" They did not.

Westcott and Hort went along 100% with the Alexandrian Text that began in Alexandria, Egypt, the headquarters of the Gnostic heretical religion. As far as his statement that Westcott and Hort "*accepted the witness of the other traditions,*" I would like to see Price, or anyone else, give me a few hundred examples of this, or even 100, or even 50, or even 25. They were "*dyed in the wool*" advocates of the "**Vatican**" ("B") manuscript, come what may. Price has but to examine the plethora of evidence favoring Mark 16:9-20 to see how these two heretics threw away all that evidence to go with their idols, the "*Vatican*" and Sinai manuscripts.

## *No Consensus of Evidence*

**STATEMENT #98.** (p. 182) "*This improved method now attempts to determine more completely the consensus of the evidence from all text traditions. Thus it is inaccurate to refer to the current form of the Westcott and Hort theory of the text as Alexandrian. However, in order to interact with the terminology used by many of the King James Only movement the term is used here when referring to current theories of textual criticism.*"

**COMMENT #98.** When Price stated "*this improved method now attempts to determine more completely the consensus of the evidence from all text traditions,*" it is a boldfaced lie! My friend, Dr. Kirk DiVietro, wrote to Bruce Metzger in 1990 and asked him how he and the other members of the Nestle/Aland and United Bible Societies Committee began their work on their New Testament text. Metzger replied in his own handwriting as follows:

> "*We took __as our base__ at the beginning __the text of Westcott and Hort__ (1881) and introduced changes as seemed necessary on the basis of MSS evidence.*" (*Dean Burgon Society 1994 Message Book*, p. 272 in BFT#2490-P]

This shows that Metzger and his other editors began with the "**Westcott and Hort**" Greek text "*as their base*." A comparison of the "*Westcott and Hort*" Greek text and the modern Nestle/Aland or United Bible Societies Text shows very, very few differences from that of Westcott and Hort which was based upon the Gnostic "*Vatican*" manuscript ("B")

It is certainly not "*inaccurate to refer to the current form of the Westcott and Hort theory of the text as Alexandrian.*" The root words of Westcott and Hort's Greek text of 1881 were from the Gnostic heretical texts of the Vatican and Sinai manuscripts. These manuscripts were corrupted in Alexandria, Egypt, which were the headquarters of the Gnostics. "*Alexandrian*" is a perfectly good and truthful term to use to refer to the "*Westcott and Hort*" false text.

# The Error of Genealogical Families

**STATEMENT #99.** (p. 182) Price has a heading called "*The Classical Method.*" He said: "*This method primarily attempts to construct a genealogical stemma of the history of a text based on the principal that apart from accident, identity of reading implies identity of origin.*"

**COMMENT #99.** I agree with Dean Burgon and others who reject completely the so-called "*genealogical stemma*." As the writers of the Bible wrote, the Words were copied accurately throughout history. The identity of that goes back to the originals, not back to a certain family. Dean Burgon opposed "*stemma*" and "*genealogy*." He said that "*genealogical*" method is false. He said every manuscript is an orphan child.

> "*The living inhabitants of a village, congregated in the churchyard where the bodies of their forgotten progenitors for 1000 years repose without memorials of any kind,* [In other words, there are no gravestones in this cemetery.]--*is a faint image of the relation which subsists between extant copies of the Gospels and the sources from which they were derived.*" [Dean John W. Burgon, *Revision Revised*, p. 256].

You can't trace manuscripts back to "*genealogy*" or "*stemma*" or families. Westcott and Hort had to dream up this so-called *"family of manuscripts"* theory, because they knew that they had only 45 manuscripts compared with the over 5,210 manuscripts of the Traditional Received Text. Westcott and Hort had to diminish these 5,210 manuscripts by inventing three *"families"* among their 45 manuscripts and one family among the 5,210. This makes a 3 to 1 decision on any given word rather than accepting the evidence of the entire 5,210 and rejecting the 45. It is a complicated argument, but it is indeed false. The manuscripts are like a cemetery with unmarked graves. You cannot be certain about the family relationship of any of those thus buried. So with the manuscripts. They form one great entire entity and as such are independent witnesses.

**STATEMENT #100.** (p. 185) *"German scholar Johann Joseph Griesbach (1745-1812) categorized the New Testament manuscripts into three families which were a result of ancient recensions: the Alexandrian, Western, and the Byzantine."*

**COMMENT #100.** *"Griesbach"* was a German higher critic apostate-unbeliever. There is no reason why Bible-believing Christians should follow him in these lies he has concocted. First of all, there are not *"three families,"* or any *"families"* at all. Every manuscript is independent of all others. Westcott and Hort and others have added a fourth so-called *"family."* Second, there is no documentary or historical proof that there were any *"ancient recensions"* at all. This is just one more lie the Critical Text fanatics have concocted to justify their empty profession of the Gnostic words from Alexandria, Egypt. Here's how Dean Burgon phrased it:

*"The living inhabitants of a village, congregated in the churchyard where the bodies of their forgotten progenitors for 1000 years repose without memorials of any kind, [In other words, there are no gravestones in this cemetery.]—is a faint image of the relation which subsists between extant copies of the Gospels and the sources from which they were derived."* [Dean Burgon, *Revision Revised*, p. 256].

# 225 of His Statements and My Comments-- Statements ##101-150

## Westcott & Hort's Text & Theory

**STATEMENT #101.** (p. 187)  Price has a heading entitled: "*Westcott and Hort Developed a New Theory*." Speaking of the Westcott and Hort Greek text of 1881, he wrote: "*The text was based on a theory of textual criticism they developed from the foundation laid by their predecessors. Their text and theory were widely accepted by many of their contemporaries, including most theological conservative scholars*."

   **COMMENT #101.**  While it is true that "*Their text and theory were widely accepted by many*," nevertheless, both their "*text*" and their "*theory*" were and are totally false. As to how many of their "*contemporaries*" were "*theologically conservative scholars*" who accepted their theory is not known. Tregelles was a conservative follower of the Plymouth Brethren who fell for this false theory. On the other hand, Dean John William Burgon, a conservative clergyman from the Church of England, wrote five major books opposing their many, many errors of fact and theory. All five of these books have been reprinted in hardback editions and are available by looking up either the **Bible For Today** at this URL (**www.BibleForToday.org**), or by looking up the Dean Burgon Society (**www.DeanBurgonSociety.org**)  Here are the five books by Dean Burgon:

> 1.  *Revision Revised* (BFT #611 @ $25.00 + $5.00 S&H).
> 2.  *The Last Twelve Verses of Mark* (BFT #1139 @ $16.00 + $5.00 S&H)
> 3.  *The Traditional Text* (BFT #1159 @ $16.00 + $5.00 S&H)
> 4.  *The Causes of Corruption* (BFT #1160 @ $15.00 + $5.00 S&H)
> 5.  *Inspiration and Interpretation* (BFT #1220 @ $25.00+ $5.00 S&H)
>
> Many of Dean John William Burgon's conservative countrymen also did not agree with Westcott and Hort. It was a new theory based wholly on hypothesis rather than fact.

# The Myth of Text-Types

**STATEMENT #102.** (p. 187) "*Westcott and Hort advocated that the genealogical relationship among manuscripts is of primary importance, and that the evidence from text-types thus identified should be evaluated on the basis of their reputation of being correct.*"

   **COMMENT #102.** There is no proven "*genealogical relationship*" between the Greek New Testament manuscripts. This is false, as Dean John W. Burgon has so adequately proved.

> There is, therefore, no such thing as "*text-types*." This is merely a necessary lie perpetrated by Westcott and Hort to deceive people into believing the total impossibility that just two Gnostic manuscripts (Vatican and Sinai) could cancel out over 5,200 others.

Here's what Dean Burgon wrote about this:
"*The living inhabitants of a village, congregated in the churchyard where the bodies of their forgotten progenitors for 1000 years repose without memorials of any kind,* [In other words, there are no gravestones in this cemetery.]*--is a faint image of the relation which subsists between extant copies of the Gospels and the sources from which they were derived.*" [Dean John W. Burgon, *Revision Revised,* p. 256].

   **STATEMENT #103.** (p. 187) "*On the basis of their investigation, they identified four principal text-types that they called the Syrian, the Western, the Alexandrian, and the Neutral. Figure 10.4 is a stemma representing their view of the genealogical relationships of the manuscripts, versions, and fathers.*"

> **COMMENT #103.** Even though "*they identified four principal text-types*," this is a myth. There is no such thing as a genealogical relationship. Each New Testament Greek manuscript is an independent source, unrelated to any other.

# Church Fathers Prove TR Not Late

**STATEMENT #104.** (pp. 188-189) "*Westcott and Hort regarded it* [the Syrian Text] *as late and unreliable* because the text was supported by no early manuscripts. It appeared to be the result of a fourth century revision. The Textus Receptus represents its latest form.*"

     **COMMENT #104.** When Price stated: "*Westcott and Hort regarded it* [the Syrian Text] *as late and unreliable*," he is giving their position, but it is dead wrong. Many of the so-called "*scholars*" of schools and seminaries (even many of those who are Fundamentalists) who follow Bishop Westcott and Professor Hort have trashed the multitudes of Traditional Received Greek manuscripts. They say that, though they are in great number, they are, as liberal Westcott and Hort said, "*late and unreliable*."

     This is a serious and oft-repeated lie. This is the reason we use the quotations or allusions of the early Church Fathers to prove that the Traditional Received Words were early, not "*late*." There are many early manuscripts that support the Words of the "*Syrian*" or "*Textus Receptus*."

>      Dean Burgon and his staff examined the quotations or allusions of 76 early Church Fathers that died 400 AD or before (See *The Traditional Text*, BFT #1159 @ $16.00 + $5.00 S&H).. He found that not only were there solid evidences of early existence of these "*Traditional Received Greek*" Words, but they were in a plurality of 3 to 2 which is 60% to 40%. Some of these Church Fathers died in 150 or 200 AD, and yet they had in their hands manuscripts that were definitely the Traditional Received kind of Text. Dr. Jack Moorman repeated this examination in our own time and found the ratio of Traditional Received Words to Critical Text words was 70% to 30%. This is found in Dr. Moorman's book: *Early Manuscripts, Church Fathers, and the Authorized Version* (BFT #3230 @ $20.00 + $5.00 S&H).

     On these two pages, Price gives the pictures of both Brooke Foss Westcott (1825-1901) and Fenton John Anthony Hort (1828-92). Westcott was an apostate heretical bishop in the Church of England who talked out of both sides of his mouth. On the one hand he sounded like a conservative. On the other hand he sounded like a liberal. He did this in order to convince both wings of his church. This was very clever on his part. Hort was an apostate professor at the University of Cambridge. These two heretics were the originators of the popular Critical Text that differs from the Traditional Received Words in more than 8,000 places. [For all of these places, see *8,000 Differences Between the Critical Text and the Traditional Text* by Dr. Jack Moorman (**BFT #3084 for a gift of $20.00 + $5.00 S&H)**]

# TR–No 4th Century Revision

**STATEMENT #105.** (p. 189) "*It appeared to be the result of a fourth century revision. The Textus Receptus represents its latest form.*"

**COMMENT #105.** There is no historical evidence or proof of any "*fourth century revision*" of the New Testament Greek text. It is therefore also false to say that the "*Textus Receptus represents its latest form.*" The facts scream out loudly that the Traditional Received Words underlying the King James Bible are in no way the product or either a 250 A.D. or a 350 A.D. "*recension*" or "*revision*" of some kind. Dean Burgon has shown that this charge has no basis in fact or history. He wrote:

> *Excuse me, I forget no such thing; and for a very good reason, because such Recensions never occurred. Why, there is not a trace of them in history: it is a mere dream of Dr. Hort: they must be 'phantom recensions,' as Dr. Scrivener terms them.*" The *Traditional Text,* by Dean John W. Burgon, p. 79 [See BFT #1159 @ $16.00 + $5.00 S&P]

If the Traditional Received Textus Receptus is late, how could the research by Dean Burgon and his staff be true? He traced 76 Church Fathers who died 400 A.D. and before. He found that not only did these church leaders have the Traditional Received Words in their hands, but they either quoted them or alluded to them 60% of the time. How could this be if this text was not in existence until some "*fourth century revision*"? [For documentation on this, see *The Traditional Text*, pp. 99-102, **BFT #1159 @ $16.00 + $5.00 S&P**]

# More About False Text-Type Stemma

**STATEMENT #106.** (p. 190) "*Figure 10.4 Westcott & Hort's Genealogical Stemma.*"

**COMMENT #106.** Price has a number of charts alleging so-called "*text types*" or "*Genealogical Stemma.*" There is no evidence that one manuscript is related to another. This is something that Westcott and Hort have made up in order to convince people that the Textus Receptus or the Traditional Text was derived from previous texts. The truth of the matter is that the Traditional Received Words were the originals and all the corrupt words were derived from them.

# Westcott & Hort Used Guesswork

**STATEMENT #107.** (p. 191) *"In addition, Westcott and Hort carefully employed internal evidence to help resolve genealogical uncertainties. These lines of evidence included: (1) Transcriptional probabilities involving the **known habits of scribes**. (2) Intrinsic probabilities involving the **known habits of the author**."*

**COMMENT #107.** How ridiculous can you get! The "**known habits of scribes**" are completely unknown. The "**known habits of the author**" are also completely unknown. Both of these "**probabilities**" are pure speculation and guesswork. This whole process is phony, false, and foolishness. How can you talk about "**probability**" and only guess what the writers of the Words of God wrote? Internal evidence is a false kind of evidence when trying to construct words of the Scripture.

The Words of the Bible must be based on external evidence such as manuscripts, early versions, quotes or allusions by the Church Fathers or similar objective evidence rather than on the thin ice of guesswork and mind-reading. Dean Burgon put it like this:

*But then we make it our fundamental rule to reason always from grounds of **external Evidence,--never from postulates of the Imagination**. (Revision Revised, p. 96)* [BFT #611 @ $25.00 + $5.00 S&H]

# Price's Phony "Recension" Theory

**STATEMENT #108.** (p. 192) Now Price takes up his phony text-family genealogical yarn. He begins with the so-called Antiochan Text, which is the alleged basis of the King James Bible. He wrote: *"It is the ancestor of the Byzantine Text which is **the result of a 4ᵗʰ Century recension** or equivalent. The Byzantine Text is supported by the majority of the manuscripts. **The Textus Receptus is a late development of that text**."*

**COMMENT #108.** This is an absolute falsehood. The Traditional Received Text is not "**the result of a 4ᵗʰ Century recension**" as Price stated. There is no historical proof of any "**recension**." The Traditional Received Words were the original Words from the Apostolic days. It was from the very beginning of the New Testament. There are thirty-seven historical links of this text down to the present. (See my book, *Defending the King James Bible*, pp. 44-48 [BFT #1594 @ $12.00 + $5.00 S&H]). It has continuity. This cannot be said for the Critical Text which died out after about *"450 A.D."* (See *Codex B and Its Allies* by Hermann Hoskier, pp. 468-469 [BFT #1643 @ $46.00 + $8.00 S&H]). Again, Price makes a totally false statement by saying that *"the Textus Receptus is a late development of that text."*

# Gnostic MSS Not "Numerous"

**STATEMENT #109.** (p. 192) Price lists the false so-called *"text types"* going from *"Antiochan," "Western," "Caesarean,"* and *"Alexandrian."* Then he comments on the *"Alexandrian Text."* He wrote: *"The Alexandrian Text corresponds to Westcott and Hort's neutral text, but more manuscripts are used to determine its readings. Besides Aleph and B, numerous other uncials, papyri, and minuscule manuscripts now bear witness to this text. The text is supported by quotations from the Egyptian Church Fathers and the Coptic and Ethiopic translations. This text is still judged by some to be the best, but due consideration is given to other witnesses."*

**COMMENT #109.** It is false for Price to say that *"Besides Aleph and B, numerous other uncials, papyri, and minuscule manuscripts now bear witness to this text."* When Price says there are *"numerous manuscripts"* that *"bear witness to this text,"* how does Price define *"numerous"*?

Out of Kurt Aland's 1967 total of 5,255 New Testament manuscripts, Dr. Jack Moorman, in his book, *Forever Settled* (BFT #1428 @ $20.00 + $5.00 S&H), beside "Aleph and B," lists only 43 others out of the 5,255. Does this seem *"numerous"* to you? Not to me. This is one of Price's biggest lies and deceptions in his book.

It is false to say that *"due consideration is given to other witnesses."* As a matter of fact, Bishop Westcott and Professor Hort needed only the Vatican ("B") manuscript to solve all their problems, or any manuscript that agreed with "B" whether it be Sinai (Aleph) or some other manuscript.

**STATEMENT #110.** (p. 193) Price has a chart that he calls *"Genealogical Stemma According to the Reasoned Eclectic Theory..."*

**COMMENT #110.** There is no such thing as a "genealogical stemma." Price's chart makes it look factual, but the fact remains, as Dean John W. Burgon has so aptly said, the manuscripts are all *"orphan children."*

*"The living inhabitants of a village, congregated in the churchyard*

*where the bodies of their forgotten progenitors for 1000 years repose without memorials of any kind,* [In other words, there are no gravestones in this cemetery.]--*is a faint image of the relation which subsists between extant copies of the Gospels and the sources from which they were derived."* [Dean John W. Burgon, *Revision Revised*, p. 256].

There is no proof whatsoever that they are genealogically linked one to another. The old saying comes to mind: *"Figures can't lie, but liars can figure."* That's exactly what this chart is, a chart of lies.

# The TR Not Late or Secondary

**STATEMENT #111.** (p. 193) *"This example illustrates the <u>late, secondary character</u> of the Byzantine Text."*

**COMMENT #111.** These are two more of Price's lies. The Traditional Received Words are neither *"<u>late</u>"* nor of *"<u>secondary character</u>."* They are *"early,"* and, as such, are of a *"primary character."*

# No Genealogical Relationship

**STATEMENT #112.** (p. 195) *"The readings of the various manuscripts are evaluated on the basis of <u>antiquity</u>, independence and <u>genealogical relationship</u>."*

**COMMENT #112.** What about the *"number"* of manuscripts? As for *"<u>antiquity</u>,"* are they looking at the age of the material the words are written on, or for the age of the words? We should be looking for the age of the words rather than the age of the material the words are written on.

> The Words of the Traditional Received Greek New Testament go all the way back to Apostolic times. Just because the materials on which these Words were written are ancient does not mean the Words themselves are ancient. For example, the Vatican "B") and the Sinai ("Aleph") manuscripts are old (4th century), but their Words were doctored by Gnostic heretics within 100 years after the New Testament was completed. The Traditional Received Words, on the other hand, were the original Words of the New Testament writers though the materials on which they are now written are older than the false manuscripts referred to above. As for the so-called *"<u>genealogical relationship</u>"* between the Greek manuscripts, there are none that are provable.

# False "Text-Type" Probabilities

**STATEMENT #113.** (p. 195) *"The readings of the various ancient text types are also evaluated on the basis of two types of internal probabilities transcriptional probabilities and intrinsic probabilities."*

**COMMENT #113.** There are two basic errors in Price's statement.

(1) The first is non-existent *"text types."* There is no such thing as *"text types"* as I have said many times earlier. Every manuscript stands alone.

(2) The second error is the term *"internal probabilities."* Any reliable researcher worth his salt does not and cannot go on such *"probabilities."* He must rely on external evidence. *"Transcriptional probabilities and intrinsic probabilities"* are pure guesswork. As Dean Burgon said of his detractors,

> *"I must really pray you to pause:–you have left facts far behind, and have mounted into cloud-land."* (*The Traditional Text*, p. 71) [BFT #1159 @ $16.00 + $5.00 S&H]

Again, Dean Burgon wrote:

> *"In contrast with this sojourn in cloud-land, we are essentially of the earth though not earthy. We are nothing, if we are not grounded in facts: our appeal is to facts, our test lies in facts, so far as we can build testimonies upon testimonies and pile facts on facts."* (p. 238)

Neither Price, nor any other textual critic, should take *"transcriptional probability"* and try to figure out what a scribe would have copied. That has nothing to do with truth. *"Intrinsic probability"* is what Bishop Westcott and Professor Hort advocated in order to try to figure out how the writers of the Bible would have written a particular passage. It ill behooves Price to seek to dabble in this line of idiocy. He's much smarter than that.

# Price Exalts the Critical Text

**STATEMENT #114.** (p. 197) *"The currently published Critical Text of the Greek New Testament follow this method for recovering the autographic text. The most widely used text is that of E. Nestle and Kurt Aland, Novum Testamentum Graece, 27ᵗʰ edition."*

**COMMENT #114.** This **Nestle/Aland** text is an erroneous Greek New Testament text that, sad to say, is used in many schools, colleges, and seminaries that call themselves "Fundamental." The text they should be using is that by Dr. :Frederick Scrivener. It can be ordered from the **Bible For Today**, 900 Park Avenue, Collingswood, NJ 08108 as **BFT #1670 @ $35.00**

+ $5.00 S&H.  It is called *Scrivener's Annotated Greek New Testament*.

# A Critical Hebrew Text Coming

**STATEMENT #115.**  (p. 205) *"Work is in progress for producing a Critical Text for a Hebrew Bible with a much better critical apparatus, yet the projects are progressing very slowly."*

> **COMMENT #115.**  How horrible! I have known of this attempt for many years now.  They are combining all the erroneous principles instead of accepting what has been given to us down through the centuries of the Traditional Received Daniel Bomberg Edition, Ben Chayyim edition, and the Hebrew and Aramaic Words underlying the King James Bible.

# Price's False "Back-Translation" View

**STATEMENT #116.**  (p. 209) *"The current Textus Receptus became stable only after it was made to conform to the English Words of the King James Version by a form of back-translation."*

> **COMMENT #116.**  Saying that the *"current Textus Receptus"* is *"a form of back-translation"* is absolute falsehood! It is one of the most ridiculous statements made by Price yet.  Where is Price's proof of this nonsense?  This is stupidity.  He is talking about the Greek text published by Dr. Frederick Scrivener's Greek text.  He was one of the greatest Greek scholar in his day.  He was a contemporary of Dean John William Burgon and one of the translators of the English Revised Version of 1881.  He was the one who was trying to hold the line for the Traditional Received Text, but was outnumbered.  Westcott and Hort were on that committee and they wanted to change the Scriptures and the Greek text.

After this was completed, Dr. Scrivener was asked by the University of Cambridge Press to publish a Greek text that underlies the King James Bible. They also wanted with that text to have the differences shown between the text that underlies the King James Bible and the Critical Text of Westcott and Hort and the English Revised Version of 1881. That is what Dr. Scrivener did. To do this, he most certainly did not *"back-translate"* from English to Greek as Price falsely has stated.

> On the contrary, he sought to find New Testament Greek editions that most closely underlie the King James Bible.  He found the closest printed edition to be that of Beza's 5th edition of 1598.  In the Appendix he cited 190 places where the King James translators chose a text other than that of Beza's 5th edition, 1598.

You can get a copy of this *Scrivener's Annotated Greek New Testament* online at **BibleForToday.org**, or by writing the **Bible For Today** at 900 Park Avenue, Collingswood, New Jersey 08108. It is **BFT #1670 @ $35.00 + $5.00 S&H**. It is an enlarged copy so you can read it much more easily. In the footnotes it shows how Westcott and Hort's Greek text and the English Revised Version of 1881 changed the Words of God. I counted 5,600 places where there were changes made. To have Price say that the text of Scrivener was "**back-translated**" from English to Greek is not only the height of stupidity, but without a shred of historical evidence to prove his false charge.

# Critical Text–No Continuity

**STATEMENT #117.** (p. 209) "*Opponents of the critical Greek New Testament object that the text contained in the critical edition is discontinuous. That is the text died out in antiquity and was not preserved down through history in a continuous line of manuscripts as was true for the Byzantine Tradition.*"

**COMMENT #117.** Though Price denies it, this statement is factually correct. The "*critical edition is discontinuous.*" Unlike the Traditional Received Text, the Critical Text is not present "*in a continuous line of manuscripts*" from the Apostolic times to the present. There are 37 historical links in the history of the Traditional Received Words. See my *Defending the King James Bible*, pp.44-48 [BFT #1594 @ $12.00 + $5.00 S&H].

> The Critical Text, on the other hand, was "*abandoned from 500 to 1881*" (See Herman Hoskier, *Codex B & Its Allies*, pp. 468-469 [BFT #1643 @ $46.00 + $8.00 S&H])

# Where Are Price's "Many Witnesses"?

**STATEMENT #118.** (p. 209) "*But many witnesses to the Critical Text have survived through the years of history and still exist so in that sense they have been preserved--existence validates preservation.*"

**COMMENT #118.** When he wrote that "*many witnesses to the Critical Text have survived through the years of history and still exist,*" Price has, once again, falsified reality. I fail to see how Price can conclude that there are "*many witnesses*" to the "*Critical Text*" that "*still exist.*"

> According to the careful research of Dr. Jack Moorman in his book, *Forever Settled* [BFT #1428 @ $20.00 + $5.00 S&H], the only "*witnesses*" to the "*Critical Text*" among Kurt Aland's manuscripts as of 1967 were the Vatican, the Sinai, and 43 others, making a total of 45. When Aland's manuscript total, at that date, was 5,255, how can Price falsely state that

45 constitutes "*many witnesses*"? How misleading can you get! The Traditional Received Words, with upwards of 5,210 manuscripts that "*still exist*," truly and correctly comprise "*many witnesses*," but not the 45 manuscripts of the "*Critical Text*."

Price has not dealt with the fact that the Critical Text is "*not continuous*," nor can he, because it has "*no continuity*" after around 500 A.D.  The two reasons that account for the preservation of the Vatican and Sinai ("B" and Aleph) manuscripts are as follows: (1) The climate of Egypt was conducive to the preservation of those two false manuscripts; (2) These manuscripts were not used very much and therefore were preserved.  The early church didn't use them because they knew them to be false.  These false manuscripts were just put on the shelf of a library, either in the Vatican or in the Sinai desert.

I have some books downstairs in my basement I have never used.  I have them, but I hardly ever open them.  For example, I have the Jehovah Witness Bible Version and Mary Baker Eddy's *Science and Health With Key to the Scriptures*.  Though they are over 70 years old, they are in perfect condition because I seldom use them.

# Price's Falsification of Evidence

**STATEMENT #119.**  (p. 210) ". . . *the 250 uncials most of which are non-Byzantine, and a group of about 60 minuscules that consistently differ from the Byzantine Text*."

**COMMENT #119.**  Price has falsified the facts once again when he spoke of "*the 250 uncials most of which are non-Byzantine*."  As a matter of fact, there are at least 267 uncials according to Kurt /Aland's figures of 1967.  A second lie is when Price stated that "*most of which are non-Byzantine*."  According to the analysis of Dr. Jack Moorman in his book, *Forever Settled* [BFT #1428 @ $20.00 + $5.00], there are only 9 manuscripts that follow the Critical Text and 258 that follow the Traditional Received Words.  You can see a chart of this on page 56 in my book, *Defending the King James Bible* [BFT #1594 @ $12.00 + $5.00 S&H].  It is a lie that most uncials are non-Byzantine.  What does Price mean by the word "*most*"?

When Price speaks of "*a group of about 60 minuscules that consistently differ from the Byzantine Text*," he has missed the target once again.  Here are the facts of the case.  According to Kurt Aland, once again, as of 1967, there were 2,741 "*minuscules*" or cursive manuscripts.  There were not "*about 60*" of them that "*differ from the Byzantine Text*," but only 23.  The other 2,741 are in accord with the Traditional Received Words.

Price is trying to make a case for the superiority of the Critical Text, but in so doing, he has given false statistics for that text which is inferior in numbers, inferior in continuity, and inferior in quality.

# Critical Text--Corrupt Doctrine+Text

**STATEMENT #120.** (p. 210) Price has a title called "*It is a Corrupt Text*." He wrote: "*The opponents of the Critical Text inappropriately demonize it as though it is full of doctrinal errors or alterations that diminish certain important doctrines*."

**COMMENT #120.** It is a fact that "*the Critical Text*" is "*full of doctrinal errors or alterations that diminish certain important doctrines*." It is full of inappropriate and false doctrines. You don't have to take my word for these "*doctrinal errors or alterations*."

You can see them for yourselves by getting Dr. Jack Moorman's book, *Early MSS, Church Fathers, & the Authorized Version* (pp. 119-312). In this book, Dr. Moorman has listed over 356 doctrinal passages where the "*Critical Text*" is doctrinally in error.

In my book, *Defending the King James Bible* [BFT #1594 @ $12.00 + $5.00 S&H], in Chapter V, I list and comment on 158 of the more important of those 356 doctrinal passages. I explain how and where the modern versions that have followed the Vatican and Sinai manuscripts have followed these doctrinal corruptions.

**STATEMENT #121.** (p. 210) "*However, these scholars use the term 'corrupt' in the sense of textual corruption not doctrinal corruption*."

**COMMENT #121.** Here again Price has spun facts into total error. When he wrote about "*textual corruption not doctrinal corruption*," he is wrong again. There is both "*textual*" and "*doctrinal corruption*" in the Critical Text and the Bible versions in languages all over the world that depend upon them.

As I have said before, there are over 8,000 "*textual*" differences in the Critical Text and over 356 doctrinal errors. For solid documentation on these important subjects, see Dr. Jack Moorman's two books, (1) *8,000 Differences Between the Critical Text and the Traditional Text* [BFT #3084 @ $20.00 + $5.00 S&H] and (2) *Early MSS, Church Fathers, & the Authorized Version*, (pp. 119-312) [BFT #3230 @ $20.00 + $5.00 S&H.] is in doctrinal error in 356 places. As usual, Price does not know what he is talking about. He is simply parroting what others have told in the lectures he has heard and the books he has read.

**STATEMENT #122.** (p. 211)  *"But some opponents have erroneously interpreted the term 'corrupt' in the doctrinal sense, claiming that the Critical Texts deny or diminish important doctrines such as the deity of Christ or the blood atonement."*

        **COMMENT #122.**  The facts of the case show that  the Critical Texts of the Vatican and Sinai are  *" 'corrupt' in the doctrinal sense"* as well as in the textual sense.  Both the *"deity of Christ"* and the *"blood atonement"* are included in the textual corruption of the Critical Texts and the Bible versions based upon them. The two above mentioned volumes prove this position conclusively.  It behooves every Bible-believing Christian to get these books, to study them, and to encourage others to do the same.

# Critical Test Diminishes Doctrine"

**STATEMENT #123.** (p. 212)  *"Regarding the deity of Christ, opponents find fault with the Critical Text for lacking the word 'Lord' referring to Jesus Christ in some places where the Textus Receptus has this word. They regard this lack as diminishing the doctrine, but that reasoning is faulty, because if the Bible records a doctrine once, the doctrine is just as true as another that is mentioned often."*

        **COMMENT #123.**    As  far  as  what  Price  called *"diminishing the doctrine,"* this is also false.  Let me illustrate some of doctrines that were *"diminished."*  In my booklet, *The Case For the Received Text of Hebrew and Greek Underlying the King James Version-- A Summary Of the Evidence & Argument* [**BFT #83** @$7.00 + $3.00 S&H], I took 162 key verses, listed them, and then classified them as to *"doctrines"* that are omitted or changed.

**Among these *"doctrines"* that are omitted or changed include:**

◆1.  the deity of Christ (sixteen verses on this);

◆2.  the omission of the Lord Jesus Christ's full title;

◆3.  the virgin birth of Christ;

◆4.  the omission of *"begotten"* which alters His eternal Sonship and His relationship with the Father;

◆5.  the omission of "Alpha and Omega" involving Christ's eternal generation and eternal future;

◆6.  the omission of Christ's omnipresence;

◆7.  the omission of Christ's eternal future state;

◆8.  the omission of Christ's part in the creation of the world;

✦9. the omission of the fact that salvation is only through genuine faith in the Lord Jesus Christ;

✦10. the weakening of the fact of Christ's bodily resurrection;

✦11. the weakening of Christ's bodily ascension;

✦12. the weakening of Christ's bodily coming again;

✦13. the weakening of Christ's great commission.

I want the doctrines named every place they are supposed to be. Once is not enough.

The reason that these Gnostic documents have cut off all or part of the complete Name of *"Lord Jesus Christ"* is because the Gnostics did not believe that the Lord Jesus Christ was one Person. They have bifurcated Him. They have stripped Him and divided Him in two. They believed He was two persons, Jesus the man, and Christ the principal of Deity. The Gnostics teach falsely that, at the baptism of Jesus, "the Christ principal" came upon Jesus, and then at the cross the Christ principal left Jesus. They believed that Jesus was only a man, not Deity. He wasn't Virgin born. He didn't perform miracles. He didn't rise from the dead. This is why the Gnostic documents split up *"Jesus"* from *"Christ."* They don't believe He is Jesus Christ. This is serious doctrinal heresy.

# Nothing Omitted? Price Was Wrong

**STATEMENT #124.** (pp. 211-212) Speaking about the Critical Text, Price said: *"Therefore, technically speaking, nothing is omitted."*

**COMMENT #124.** How can Price say *"nothing is omitted"* from the Critical Text? This is certainly false. Once again, a book by Dr. Jack Moorman comes to the rescue with documentation on this. He documented the omissions in his excellent book, *Missing in Modern Bibles–Is The True Story Being Told*? [BFT #1726 @ $8.00 + $4.00 S&H].

In preparation for this document, Dr. Moorman counted and examined both the Nestle/Aland Critical Greek Text and compared it with the Scrivener's Greek text that underlies the King James Bible. He went through every verse, from Matthew through Revelation and found a total of 2,886 Greek words that were completely missing in the Nestle/Aland Critical Greek text.

# Price's Half-Hearted Correction

**STATEMENT #125.** (p. 213) After making the previous statement quoted in **STATEMENT #124** above, Price puts in the following footnote: "*This statement is not completely true for the UBS Critical Text because it does not note all the places where textual variation takes place. It is limited to these places the editors thought were significant for translators.*"

**COMMENT #125.** Price qualifies his above statement, but still did not take it back, as he should have, his statement that "*nothing is omitted*." Last time I checked my math, 2,886 Greek Words do not add up to "*nothing*."

# Price Doubts CT Liberal Editors

**STATEMENT #126.** (p. 215) Price's caption is "*It has Unholy Editors.*" He then seeks to answer this objection: "*Some people oppose the Critical Text because some of its editors, past and present, were allegedly theologically liberal, or belonged to an unacceptable denomination, or held intolerable political views, or investigated objectionable subjects.*"

**COMMENT #126.** Let's just look at Price's leading accusation against the Critical Text that "*some of its editors, past and present, were allegedly theologically liberal.*" This is true, beginning with the two founders of this popular Critical Text in 1881, Bishop Westcott and Professor Hort. Though some Fundamentalists have written books in which they defend Anglican Westcott and Anglican Hort as "*conservative,*" they are totally in error. They were both religious apostates and heretics.

> In my book, *The Theological Heresies of Westcott and Hort* [BFT #595 @ $7.00 + $3.00 S&H], I looked at five books, three by Westcott and two by Hort. I cited about 125 quotations to show their heresies and apostasy. After this, I also wrote another book called, *Bishop Westcott's Clever Denial of the Bodily Resurrection of Christ* [BFT #1131 @ $4.00 + $3.00 S&H]. In this book, I quote from two of Westcott's books showing that he nowhere affirms the bodily resurrection of the Lord Jesus Christ and, as such, is therefore an apostate heretic.

Kurt Aland and Bruce Metzger, who were editors of modern Critical Texts were also theological liberals.

# No Fallacious *Ad Hominem* Attacks

**STATEMENT #127.** (p. 216) *"Fortunately, not all advocates of the Textus Receptus are deceived by such a fallacious ad hominem attack."*

**COMMENT #127.** I do not believe in a *"fallacious ad hominem attack."* First of all, I believe my attacks should be true and not *"fallacious."* Second, I believe the attack should be on the person's facts, ideas, theology and beliefs rather than on his person. Price confuses attacks on a man's theological position and attacks on his person. The two books I mentioned in the above section are strong and true attacks on the beliefs and theological heresies of Westcott and Hort, not on their persons. This is a valid and necessary type of attack on these two unbelievers, just as this book is a valid and necessary attack on Price's errors in facts and judgment.

# Critical Text Pastors & Scholars

**STATEMENT #128.** (p. 216) *"The fallacious rejection of the Critical Text (based on an ad hominem attack on its editors) overlooks the other side of the coin; most fundamental and conservative pastors and scholars of the past 150 years have accepted the Critical Text, and the theory behind it without losing their love and respect for the King James Version."*

**COMMENT #128.** I do not have a *"fallacious rejection of the Critical Text,"* but rather a true and factual *"rejection"* of it. It is not based on Price's alleged *"ad hominem attack on its editors,"* but on a truthful attack on the beliefs, theologies, and alleged facts of the *"editors."* Though perhaps not completely true, it is sad to hear Price's statement that *"most fundamental and conservative pastors and scholars of the past 150 years have accepted the Critical Text, and the theory behind it."* No matter how many of these people *"accepted the Critical Text, and the theory behind it,"* it is an erroneous position based upon many untruths and fallacies.

> To claim to have a *"love and respect for the King James Version"* and yet hold strongly to the Critical Text (either of Westcott and Hort, Nestle/Aland, or the United Bible Societies) is both inconsistent and hypercritical. How can there be people who are informed about the differences in the foundational New Testament texts of the Critical Text and the Traditional Received Text *"love and respect"* them both? As I have said many times earlier in this book, the Critical Text differs from the Traditional Received Text of the King James Bible in over 8,000 places (See *8,000 Differences Between the Critical Text and the Traditional Text* by Dr. Jack Moorman [BFT #3084 @ $20.00 + $5.00 S&H]).

How can anyone have genuine and honest "*love and respect*" for New Testaments whose foundations differ in over 8,000 Greek words? Remember also that the "*Critical Text*" has been found to contain over 356 doctrinal passages that are in theological error (See *Early Manuscripts, Church Fathers, and the Authorized Version*, pages 119-312 by Dr. Jack Moorman [BFT #3230 @ $20.00 + $5.00 S&H.]). Let me repeat my question again, how can genuine and honest "*love and respect*" for New Testaments whose foundations differ in over 356 doctrinal places?

# Liberal Bias Makes Liberal Decisions

**STATEMENT #129.**    (p. 216) In Prices's footnote #88, he wrote: "*The soundness of the methodology convinced the early conservatives, in spite of the liberal views of some textual scholars. It is naive to suppose that the theological liberal bias of some textual scholars has not affected some of their decisions, but an unbiased use of sound methodology enables one to detect and filter out liberal bias.*"

**COMMENT #129.** I commend Price for admitting: "*It is naive to suppose that the theological liberal bias of some textual scholars has not affected some of their decisions*." However, his next statement is easier said than done. He wrote: "*an unbiased use of sound methodology enables one to detect and filter out liberal bias*." How can Bible-believing Christians who have accepted the critical Greek text get this "*sound methodology*"? They don't wish to learn such "*sound methodology*" offered by Dean John W. Burgon, for example.

Conservative writers in books such as *From the Mind of God to the Mind of Man, God's Word in Our Hands, Bible Preservation and Providence of God*, and *God's Word Preserved* are all totally and woefully ignorant of two major facts:

(1) that there are over 8,000 differences between the critical Greek text and the Traditional Received Text rather than just a few;

(2) that there are over 356 doctrinal passages in the Critical Text which are theologically aberrant rather than just a few or not a single one. The ignorance or non-acceptance of these two facts make it completely impossible for Bible-believing men to have any possible ability "*to detect and filter out liberal bias.*"

# Opponents–"Naively Uninformed"

**STATEMENT #130.** (p. 217) Price wrote: "*It is the naively uninformed who are susceptible to these unfounded arguments.*"

**COMMENT #130.** I am sure that Price thinks that I am a part of "*the naively uninformed.*" The fact of the matter is that both of us are approaching the Bible from different points of view. He believes that I am "*uninformed*" about the Bible issues, though I am not. I believe he is "*uninformed*" about many of the Bible issues as evidenced by many of the things he has written in this book. My arguments against the Critical Text are not "*unfounded arguments.*" They are based upon solid facts.

# Retaining the Critical Text?

**STATEMENT #131.** (p. 217) ". . . one can see *the importance of retaining the Critical Text* and its underlying Reasoned Eclectic Method as a viable option, remembering to evaluate the decisions of the editors with wise discernment.*"

**COMMENT #131.** Price is dead wrong in proclaiming "*the importance of retaining the Critical Text.*" It is the most foolish and ridiculous text that anyone could believe and receive. Though I used to accept it out of ignorance, I have found sound theological and logical reasons for rejecting it.

# Westcott and Hort Still Honored

**STATEMENT #132.** (p. 219) Price's Chapter 11 is called: "*Some Recognize the Majority Text as the Preserved Text.*" Price wrote: "*The Alexandrian tradition was essentially recognized as the authoritative text by Westcott and Hort. This statement, of course, is an oversimplification of the case. Those who have followed in their tradition have improved their theory and methodology.*"

**COMMENT #132.** There is no doubt about it that the "*Alexandrian tradition*" of the Vatican and Sinai manuscripts was "*the authoritative text by Westcott and Hort.*" This is by no means "*an oversimplification,*" but a solid fact. It is a misleading statement for Price to say that "*Those who have followed in their tradition have improved their theory and methodology.*" This implies major changes in their "*theory and methodology*" when in fact little change has been made. Worshipers of "*Westcott and Hort's*" text, theory, and methodology still begin with manuscript "B" (the Vatican) and any manuscripts that are in agreement and rule other manuscripts out as unacceptable.

> Bruce Metzger, one of the editors of the Nestle/Aland and the United Bible Societies Greek texts, boldly stated to Dr. Kirk DiVietro that, for both of these Greek editions:
>
> *"WE TOOK AS OUR BASE AT THE BEGINNING THE TEXT OF WESTCOTT AND HORT (1881) and introduced changes as seemed necessary on the basis of MSS evidence."*

This is from a letter in 1994, re-printed in the *Dean Burgon Society 1994 Message Book* (**BFT #2490-P, p. 272**). This certainly sounds like the modern Greek text revisers thoroughly admired the text, theory, and methodology of these theological heretics and adopted almost 100% of their Greek New Testament Text.

# Byzantine Text Is Textus Receptus

**STATEMENT #133.** (p. 219) *"Advocates of the Textus Receptus sometimes erroneously equate that text with the Byzantine Text. Although the two texts are quite similar they differ in hundreds of details. The Textus Receptus view is discussed in Chapter 12."*

**COMMENT #133.** *"The Byzantine Text* is just another name for the *"Textus Receptus."* Price is attempting to equate the *"Byzantine Text"* with the so-called *"Majority Text"* which is not a majority of anything. The *"Byzantine Text"* is the text that was popular during the Byzantine Empire for centuries. It is another name for the *"Textus Receptus."*

# Price's Hebrew Majority Text

**STATEMENT #134.** (p. 220) There is a caption entitled: *"The Masoretic Text is the Hebrew Majority Text."* Price wrote: *"The difference between the Traditional Text (Textus Receptus) and the Majority Text for the Hebrew Bible is minute."*

**COMMENT #134.** The Hebrew Old Testament to use is that which underlies the King James Bible. It is the Daniel Bomberg edition of 1524-25 which was the standard for the next 400 years.

# Critical Text Is The Vatican MS

**STATEMENT #135.** (p. 222) *"Critical Greek New Testaments, on the other hand, contain, in the main body of the text, words drawn from a variety of manuscripts. The Critical Text itself is not found in any one particular Greek Manuscript."*

COMMENT #135. Price is wrong when he stated that "*the Critical Text itself is not found in any one particular Greek Manuscript*." For all intents and purposes and without much variation, it is taken from the Vatican manuscript, "B" and from one of the 43 other manuscripts that agree with "B." The Critical Text has just a minute, dwarf-like group of manuscript authority. It is limited to the Vatican and Sinai manuscripts and 43 others that agree. This is less than 1% of the surviving evidence. This is contrasted to the more than 5,210 manuscripts on which the Traditional Received Words are based. This is over 99% of the surviving evidence. It is indeed pathetic how so many otherwise Fundamental men have fallen into the liberal and idolatrous worship of this less than 1% of the evidence!

# Bomberg Hebrew vs. BHS Hebrew

STATEMENT #136. (p. 222)  Price's footnote #6 states:  "*As the executive editor of the New King James Old Testament, Chairman of the executive review committee for that version, I had the opportunity to examine the text of the Bomberg and BHS in every place where a question of translation came up. I recorded only the nine differences listed above. If others exist I have not noticed them. Advocates of the King James Only view proclaim that there are many differences and have challenged the results of my comparison and have not produced any further differences that would affect translation.*"

COMMENT #136.  As to Price's false assertion that those who differ with him "*have not produced any further differences that would affect translation*," let me say this. The Daniel Bomberg Hebrew text did not have 15 to 20 footnotes on every page of his text as the "*BHS*" *Biblia Hebraica* has. This "*BHS*" Hebrew text suggests from 20,000 to 30,000 changes that could very well be made in the Hebrew Words. If these changes were actually made in the Hebrew Words (as modern versions such as the NIV has done), it "*would affect translation*" as the NIV has done.

# Burgon Did Not Like "Majority Text"

STATEMENT #137. (p. 223)  Price has a caption that says, "*John W. Burgon preferred the Greek Majority Text.*"

COMMENT #137.  That is a false statement. Dean "*John W. Burgon*" never used the "*Majority Text*" for his preferred text. Here is what Dean Burgon called his text:

"*XIII. The one great Fact, which especially troubles him and his joint Editor,--(as well it may)--is The Traditional Greek Text of* *the New Testament Scriptures. Call this Text **Erasmian** or **Complutensian**,--the Text of **Stephens**, or of **Beza**, or of the **Elzevirs**,--call it the 'Received,' or the **Traditional Greek Text**, or **whatever other name you please**;--the fact remains, that a Text has come down to us **which is attested by a general consensus of ancient Copies, ancient Fathers, ancient Versions**. This, at all events, is a point on which, (happily,) there exists entire conformity of opinion between Dr. Hort and ourselves. Our Readers cannot have yet forgotten his virtual admission that,--Beyond all question the **Textus Receptus** is the dominant Graeco-Syrian Text of A.D. 350 to A.D. 400. Obtained from a variety of sources, this Text proves to be essentially the same in all."* [*The Revision Revised* by Dean John W. Burgon, p. 269]

---

You will note here there are eight different names plus a general name for this historic text from Apostolic times. Dean Burgon never once called it the "*Greek Majority Text*." This is an outright lie that tries to put Dean Burgon on Price's side with some form of the present so-called "*Majority Text*" of either Hodges and Farstad or Robinson-Pierpont. Neither of these conflicting "*Majority Texts*" followed Dean Burgon's very clear method of bringing the Textus Receptus up-to-date in the few places where he thought it might be needed. For a summary of his precise methods, I encourage the reader to get a copy of my book, *Burgon's Warning on Revision* (BFT #804 @ $7.00 + $3.00 S&H).

---

# Burgon's *Last Twelve Verses of Mark*

**STATEMENT #138.** (p. 223) In Price's Footnote #7, he cites "John W. Burgon, *The Last Twelve Verses of Mark Vindicated Against Recent Critical Objectors and Established*.

**COMMENT #138.** Price cited the publisher as "(*London: James Parker and Co., 1871*)." No one can get this book from London because it has been out of print for many years. If Price really wanted his readers to obtain this excellent book, he could have put in the address (which I am sure he knows) of the Dean Burgon Society at Box 354, Collingswood, New Jersey 08108. It is **BFT #1139 @ $15.00 + $5.00 S&H.** People can obtain this book and the other three of Burgon's books that Price cites, at this same address. Each of these four books will turn readers away from either the Critical Text or the so-called "*Majority Text*" that Price raves about. Perhaps for this reason, Price has not disclosed where they can be obtained.

# Burgon For The Textus Receptus

**STATEMENT #139.** (p. 223) Referring to Dean Burgon, Edward Miller, and Dr. Frederick Scrivener, Price wrote: *"These men referred to the text they exposed as the Traditional Text, but they used the term in a different sense than that used by the advocates of the Textus Receptus."*

                     **COMMENT #139.** When Price said that these men *"used the term in a different sense than that used by the advocates of the Textus Receptus,"* this is false. Look again at Dean Burgon's quotation from page 269 of his Traditional Text cited above under **STATEMENT #137.** It is a text *"which is attested by a general consensus of ancient Copies, ancient Fathers, ancient Versions."* This can be said of the Textus Receptus as much as of the Traditional Text. Remember Burgon's quote above. Notice how he talks about the *"Textus Receptus"* and remember it well when Price seeks to separate himself and to disparage the term:

> *"Beyond all question the **Textus Receptus** is the dominant Graeco-Syrian Text of* A.D. *350 to* A.D. *400. Obtained from a variety of sources, this Text proves to be essentially the same in all."* [*The Revision Revised* by Dean John W. Burgon, p. 269]

# Price's Quote Of An Error

**STATEMENT #140.** (p. 224) Price gives a quotation from Edward Miller who was a close associate of Dean Burgon, *"First, be it understood that we do not advocate perfection in the Textus Receptus. We allow that here and there it requires **revision**. In the text left behind by **Dean Burgon**, about 150 corrections have been suggested by him in St. Matthew's gospels alone."*

                     **COMMENT #140.** That is not a true statement. If you examine Miller's book where he takes this matter up, many of the citations he uses are not those of *"**Dean Burgon**,"* but of other people.

While Dean Burgon said there were slight changes that might be made in the Textus Receptus as it then stood, he also said that you should not make any major corrections or *"**revision**"* in it without first looking at:

        ✦(1) all the uncials (capital letter manuscripts),

        ✦(2) all the cursives (small letter cursives),

        ✦(3) all the lectionaries,

        ✦(4) all the early translations or versions, and

        ✦(5) all the quotations or allusions of the Church Fathers.

Only when you do it ALL should you make any *"**revision**"* to the Textus

Receptus. Again, I suggest to the reader to get my book, *Burgon's Warning on Revision* (**BFT #804 @ $7.00 + $3.00 S&H**) and see exactly Dean Burgon's warnings against "*revision*" of the Textus Receptus without first meeting ALL his detailed requirements. The Critical Text did not meet them and the so-called "*Majority Texts*" do not meet them either.

# Majority Text Vs. Textus Receptus

**STATEMENT #141.** (p. 224)  Referring to his so-called "*Majority Text*," Price wrote: "*As pointed out later in Chapter 12, this text differs from the Textus Receptus in hundreds of places*."

**COMMENT #141.**  Dean Burgon made allowances for some differences, but he did not want to make up his mind definitively until all of the safeguards were followed as I have summed them up in *Burgon's Warning on Revision* (**BFT #804 @ $7.00 + $3.00 S&H**).

# Antiquity OK–If All Things Are Equal

**STATEMENT #142.** (p. 225)  Price had a caption, referring to Dean Burgon: "*His Test of Antiquity*." Price wrote of this: "*This note of truth* [that is Dean Burgon's notes of truth] *is based on the observation that accidental and deliberate variations are propagated through subsequent copies, and that new variations which accumulate randomly in succeeding copies are likewise propagated. Consequently within a text tradition, all things being equal, the manuscript nearest the age of the autographs will have the least number of accumulated variants and variations*."

**COMMENT #142.**  Notice carefully what Price is saying under the "*Test of Antiquity*." He said: "*Consequently within a text tradition all things being equal the manuscript nearest the age of the autographs will have the least number of accumulated variants and variations*." Notice that he said "*all things being equal*." But all things were not "*equal*" because the Gnostic heretics from Alexandria, Egypt, altered their Vatican and Sinai manuscripts in thousands of places to conform to their false doctrines.

I wonder why Price did not quote the following from Dean Burgon on the "*Test of Antiquity*"?

---

**THE SEVEN NOTES OF TRUTH.**

**§ 1. _Antiquity_.**

*"The more ancient testimony is probably the better testimony. That it is not by any means always so is a familiar fact. To quote the known dictum of a competent judge:* [Dr. Frederick Scrivener] *'It is no less true to fact than paradoxical in sound, that the worst corruptions to which the New Testament has ever been subjected, originated within a hundred years after it was composed; that Irenaeus and the African Fathers and the whole Western, with a portion of the Syriac Church, used far inferior manuscripts to those employed by Stunica, or Erasmus, or Stephen, thirteen centuries after, when moulding the Textus Receptus:' Therefore* _Antiquity alone affords no security that the manuscript in our hands is not infected with the corruption which sprang up largely in the first and second centuries._*"* [Dean Burgon, *The Traditional Text*, p. 40]

---

This quotation sets the record straight as to Dean Burgon's true feelings regarding "_antiquity_" as a "*test of truth.*"

## Oldest MSS Corrupt & Unreliable

**STATEMENT #143.**  (p. 226)  *"Burgon claimed to honor the witnesses of antiquity, but he did so in a very strange way. He began by asserting **the corrupt and unreliable character of the oldest Greek manuscripts**, and then by asserting the superiority and reliability of the ancient versions and early patristic citations. He regarded the ancient versions and the patristic citations to be superior to anyone of the oldest manuscripts as a witness to the autographic text of the New Testament."*

**COMMENT #143.**  Read the preceding quotation by Dean Burgon.  What's wrong with pointing our "_the corrupt and unreliable character of the oldest Greek manuscripts_"?  It's a good caution against making "_antiquity_" the most important of the "*tests of truth.*"  The reason Burgon appreciated either the early versions or the quotations of the early church leaders is that they were dated, whereas the manuscripts are not dated. This shows which Words were present in the original manuscripts.

**STATEMENT #144.**  (p. 226)  *"Burgon and his present-day followers attempt to prove the ancient manuscript are **corrupt and unreliable** by the following line of reasoning: (1) They assert that 'antiquity does not assure purity' because the ancient manuscript may be a very poor copy of a bad form of the text and a late manuscript may be a faithful copy of an ancient* *good form of the text."*

> **COMMENT #144.** This argument is factually true. The Gnostic heretics "*corrupted*" the Vatican and Sinai manuscripts, changing them in over 8,000 places. Over 356 false doctrinal passages are involved in these changes. These doctrinal changes have conformed these two manuscripts (and the forty-three others that agree with them) to the heretical views of the Gnostic religion of ancient Alexandria, Egypt.

# Not Hasty And Unwarranted

**STATEMENT #145.** (p. 227) *"This conclusion is hasty and unwarranted, involving a logical fallacy known as circular reasoning, or assuming a conclusion."*

**STATEMENT #145.** The superiority of the Traditional Received Words of the New Testament Greek text is neither "*hasty and unwarranted*." It is based on a very old, long, and accurate array of facts which cannot be denied by Price's recitation of an old, and inappropriate, logical fallacy.

# Oldest Not Necessarily The Best

**STATEMENT #146.** (p. 227) *"The test of antiquity merely asserts that the oldest manuscripts are more likely to be faithful representatives of a text tradition than are the later ones."*

**COMMENT #146.** It is flawed to make the simple statement that "*the oldest manuscripts*" are necessarily the closest to the original Words. This completely buries the clear facts of the hundreds of Gnostic heresies found within the Vatican and Sinai manuscripts that have been repeated in the modern versions. They were early, but they were corrupted and hence are not pure but polluted. As Dean Burgon wrote:

> "*Therefore Antiquity alone affords no security that the manuscript in our hands is not infected with the corruption which sprang up largely in the first and second centuries.*" [*The Traditional Text*, p. 40]

# Critical Text Not Orthodox

**STATEMENT #147.** (p. 227) Price wrote, on footnote #18, *"Burgon used the term 'corrupt' in connection with the condition of the text-- that is, the manuscripts have variations from what he regarded as a better form of the text. . . . The overall teaching of any ancient manuscript, regarding the* *cardinal doctrines of Christianity, is found to be orthodox. Perhaps an individual passage may be a weaker expression of a given doctrine that is found in the Traditional Text, but it rarely, if ever, amounts to a denial of the given doctrine."*

**COMMENT #147.** To say *"the overall teaching of any ancient manuscript, regarding the cardinal doctrines of Christianity, is found to be orthodox,"* is totally false. Dr. Jack Moorman will show Price 356 reasons why his *"ancient manuscripts"* of Vatican and Sinai are anything but *"orthodox."* [Look at pages 119-312 of Dr. Moorman's *Early Manuscripts, Church Fathers, and the Authorized Version.* It is **BFT #3230** @ **$20.00** + **$5.00 S&H.**] These manuscripts are heretical and Price should have the honesty to admit it rather than seeking to talk his way around it.

# No Genealogical Principles In MSS

**STATEMENT #148.** (p. 231) *"Burgon's test of catholicity is nothing more than a subtle effort to avoid Westcott and Hort's **genealogical principle** that identifies several ancient text traditions and that **isolates the Byzantine Text to a single secondary witness**."*

**COMMENT #148.** There is no such thing as a *"genealogical principle."* This is an error. This is a figment of Hort's imagination in order to make less than 1% of the evidence become superior over the more than 99% of the evidence. Dean Burgon had it right that every Greek New Testament manuscript is an orphan child, independent and not related to any other. No one can prove otherwise. Dean Burgon described the Greek New Testament manuscripts in this graphic picture:

> *"The living inhabitants of a village, congregated in the churchyard where the bodies of their forgotten progenitors for 1000 years repose without memorials of any kind,* [In other words, there are no gravestones in this cemetery.]*--is a faint image of the relation which subsists between extant copies of the Gospels and the sources from which they were derived."* [Dean John W. Burgon, *Revision Revised,* p. 256].

As for there being anything that *"isolates the Byzantine Text to a single secondary witness,"* let me say this. This Traditional Received Text (to change the word, *"Byzantine"*) is not by any means *"single."* There are over 5,200 surviving Greek manuscripts of the Traditional Received Text variety. Last time I was in math class, this is by no means *"single."* Because of its being over 99% of the evidence, since when is it considered a *"secondary witness"*? It is, by all means, a *"primary witness."*

# The Critical Text Has No Continuity

**STATEMENT #149.** (p. 234) Price quotes Dean Burgon once again under the caption of "*His Test of Continuity*." He wrote: "*When therefore, a reading is observed to leave traces of its existence and of its use all down the ages, it comes with an authority of a particularly peculiarly commanding nature. And on the contrary, when a chasm of greater or less breadth of years yawns in the vast mass of evidence which is ready for employment, or when a tradition is found to have died out, upon such a fact alone suspicion or grave doubt or rejection must inevitably ensue.*"

**COMMENT #149.** I would have to agree with this accurate quotation Price made of Dean John W. Burgon. Burgon has said it all. The Critical Text has no "*continuity*" after around 500 A.D. It just stops in history. Not so with the Traditional Received Words. They have been copied and recopied from the Apostolic age to the present. [See *Defending the King James Bible*, pp.44-48 [**BFT #1594** @ $12.00 + $5.00 S&H] for 37 historical checkpoints.  What Dean Burgon is saying is that "*continuity*" is important. It's paramount.

> Here is some of the rest of Dean Burgon's quotation about the "*continuity*" of the Traditional Received Text:
>
> "*When therefore a reading is observed to leave traces of its existence and of its use all down the ages, it comes with an authority of a peculiarly commanding nature.  And on the contrary, when a chasm of greater or less breadth of years yawns in the vast mass of evidence which is ready for employment, or when a tradition is found to have died out, upon such a fact alone suspicion or grave doubt, or rejection must inevitably ensue.*
>
> *Still more, when upon the admission of the Advocates of the opinions which we are opposing the chasm is no longer restricted but engulfs not less than fifteen centuries in its hungry abyss, or else when the transmission ceased after four centuries, it is evident that according to an essential Note of Truth, those opinions cannot fail to be self-destroyed as well as to labour under condemnation during more than three quarters of the accomplished life of Christendom.*" (Dean John W. Burgon, *The Traditional Text*, p. 59 [**BFT #1159** @ $16.00 + $5.00 S&H]

The Words from the text of the Apostolic time all the way down to the present time were copied and recopied.  That is what the Critical Text lacks.

That is why Price must be against this simple continuity principle. Price can't agree with it because his Critical Text has no continuity.

> This is one of Dean Burgon's "Eight Points of Truth" – No "continuity" means the early churches didn't believe it was true so they didn't recopy it.

# There Was No "Lucian Recension"

**STATEMENT #150.** (p. 241) Price's caption is, "*The Lucian Recension Has Historical Support*."

**COMMENT #150.** This is patently false. Just because Price restates his position on the alleged "*recension*" of the New Testament Greek text, such restatement does not make it true. This is pure worship of the lies about this as told by Bishop Westcott and Professor Hort. Dean Burgon has answered this false fairy tale in many places in his book, *The Revision Revised*. Here are a few quotations of this spurious "*recension*" that allegedly took place in 250 A.D. or 350 A.D. Burgon wrote:

> "*But then, since not a shadow of proof is forthcoming that any such Recension as Dr. Hort imagines ever took place at all,---what else but a purely gratuitous exercise of the imaginative faculty is it, that Dr. Hort should proceed further to invent the method which might, or could, or would, or should have been pursued, if it had taken place? Having, however, in this way (1) Assumed a 'Syrian Recension,'--(2) Invented the cause of it,-and (3) Dreamed the process by which it was carried into execution,--the Critic hastens, more so, to characterize the historical result in the following terms: . . .*" [Dean John W. Burgon, *The Revision Revised*, pp. 273-274]

Here's another quotation from Dean Burgon:

> "*A careful. study of his book convinces me that his theory of a Syrian Recension, manufactured between A.D. 250 and A.D. 350, is a dream, pure and simple--a mere phantom of the brain.*" [*The Revision Revised*, p. 393]

> When the Nicene Creed was written, it was done at the Council of Nicea around 325 A.D. There were also several Councils of Constantinople. But, despite what Price has concocted in his own mind, there was no Council of Lucian in either the sacred records or the secular records. Price is trying to prove that this happened, but it did not happen. Price's quotations do not prove that any "*recension*" ever took place.

# 225 of His Statements and My Comments-- Statements ##151-200

## Evidence Not Examined Fully

**STATEMENT #151.** (p. 246) *"Not all of the Byzantine Manuscripts have been __examined, collated, and tabulated__."*

        **COMMENT #151.** That is true, they haven't been. *"__examined, collated, and tabulated__"* and they never will be. It is too massive an undertaking. It certainly won't be done by Dan Wallace of Dallas Theological Seminary, in spite of the hundreds of thousands of dollars he is attempting to raise for his various trips to view and record the manuscripts. That's why Dean Burgon stated that no revision of the Traditional Text should be made until **ALL** pertinent data has been inspected and *"__examined, collated, and tabulated__."* This has not been done, nor will it ever be done. Therefore, as Dean Burgon believes, just leave it alone as it stands.

## Price's Text-Type Nonsense Again

**STATEMENT #152.** (p. 247) *"On the other hand, the Byzantine Text is a __hypothetical archetype__ of the Byzantine group of manuscripts just like the Alexandrian and Western __text-types__ are __hypothetical archetypes__ of the Alexandrian and Western manuscripts."*

        **COMMENT #152.** Price's *"__hypothetical archetype__"* is only that: *"__hypothetical__."* There are no *"__text-types__"* of any kind, either Byzantine, Western, Alexandrian, or any other! No amount of repetition of talk about such phantoms will make them come to life. Each manuscript of the Greek New Testament is a lone witness and not a member of any *"__family__"* or *"__text-type__."* Let me remind the reader again of Dean Burgon's true picture of the "*relation*" between the manuscripts:

> "*The living inhabitants of a village, congregated in the churchyard where the bodies of their forgotten progenitors for 1000 years repose without memorials of any kind,* [In other words, there are no gravestones in this cemetery.]--*is a faint image of the **relation** which subsists between extant copies of the Gospels and the sources from which they were derived.*" [Dean John W. Burgon, *Revision Revised,* p. 256].

## Critical Text Contains Much Heresy

**STATEMENT #153.** (p. 249) "*In the popular representation of the Alexandrian Text, the text is associated with heresy and doctrinal corruption conveying negative implications when used in this context.*"

**COMMENT #153.** Though Price doesn't believe it, his statement about the Alexandrian text of the Vatican and Sinai manuscripts is true: "*The text is associated with heresy and doctrinal corruption.*" The reason for this is that there are over 356 doctrinal passages in this text that are false in doctrine and are therefore heretical. For all 356 of these passages, see pages 119-312 of Dr. Jack Moorman's book, *Early MSS, Church Fathers, & the Authorized Version* (**BFT #3230** @ **$20.00 + $5.00 S&H.**)] Because of this "*doctrinal corruption*" and "*heresy*," I oppose this text fervently.

**STATEMENT #154.** (p. 249) "*Chapter 15 demonstrates the translations of the Critical Text do not deny or distort any major orthodox doctrine, but are sound enough to determine good theology.*"

**COMMENT #154.** That is totally completely false. Let me quote again the following:

> "*For all 356 of these passages, see pages 119-312 of Dr. Jack Moorman's book, Early MSS, Church Fathers, & the Authorized Version (**BFT #3230** @ $20.00 + $5.00 S&H.)]*"

I would urge Price to consult Chapter V of my book, Defending the King James Bible [**BFT #1594** @ $12.00 + $5.00 S&H]. He can see 158 of these 356 doctrinal passages where the Gnostic Critical Text followed by the NIV, the NASV, the ESV, the RSV, the NRSV, and many others "*distort any major orthodox doctrine.*" Price is simply ignorant of the facts about these 356 doctrinal passage and should not be writing as he does about it, thus promoting falsehood and deceit.

# The TR Is Called Byzantine By Some

**STATEMENT #155.** (pp. 251-252) Price's Chapter 12 is entitled: "*The Traditional Text.*" He wrote: "*__The Textus Receptus is sometimes equated with the Byzantine Text__, but this equation is an error. Although the two texts are quite similar they differ in hundreds of details. The Textus Receptus is the subject of this chapter.*"

**COMMENT #155.** As I have written above under **COMMENT #133,**

> "*__The Byzantine Text__ is just another name for the "__Textus Receptus__.*" Price is attempting to equate the "*__Byzantine Text__*" with the so-called "*__Majority Text__*" which is not a majority of anything. The "*__Byzantine Text__*" is the text that was popular during the Byzantine Empire for centuries."

The "*Textus Receptus*" is certainly not exactly the same as the "*__Majority Text__*" accepted by Price. There are about 1,800 differences. This is true, but historically the "*__Byzantine Text__*" is the historical Greek text has been "*__Received__*" by all in the early years. Hence, what is wrong with calling it one form of the "*__Received__*" or "*__Textus Receptus__*"? Zane Hodges, for example, called this text the "*__Textus Receptus__*" in his notes for many years until he changed the term to the "*__Majority Text__*." It is an argument about definitions of terms rather than an argument of substance.

# KJB O.T. Was The Bomberg Hebrew

**STATEMENT #156.** (p. 254) "*Thus it was the Textus Receptus of the Hebrew Old Testament. __This edition__ and the __Complutensian Polyglot__ were the Hebrew Bibles used by the translators of the King James Version 1611.*"

**COMMENT #156.** I agree with Price that the "*__Bomberg Rabbinic Bible__*" (referred to here as "*__This edition__*") was the standard Hebrew text until 1937, as he says on this page. I disagree, however, that the King James translators used the "*__Complutensian Polyglot__*" on an equal basis with Bomberg as he seems to imply.

# KJB Used Exact Hebrew Words

**STATEMENT #157.** (p. 254) "*To this day, no printed edition of the Hebrew Bible contains the __exact Hebrew words__ behind the English words of the King James Version of 1611.*"

---

COMMENT #157. I believe that the Hebrew and Aramaic Old Testament "*Words*" that underlie the King James Bible are the "*exact Hebrew words*" that God has Preserved for us unto this day.

---

# Erasmus Used Hundreds of MSS

STATEMENT #158. (pp. 255-256) Speaking of Erasmus, Price said: "*His opportunity came when publisher Johann Froben proposed the publication of a Greek New Testament. Erasmus went to Basil in 1515 and began the editorial process with six Greek manuscripts.*"

COMMENT #158. This statement that Erasmus has only "*six Greek manuscripts*" is false and misleading. As a matter of fact, before he began his Greek New Testament, he not only had at least **ten** manuscripts in his hand, rather than only "*six.*" He also had access to all of the libraries in Europe. He visited them and examined hundreds of manuscripts. He had full access to readings of the the Vatican manuscript and rejected the readings that did not conform to the Traditional Text.

# The KJB N.T. Text Not "Hybrid"

STATEMENT #159. (p. 259) "*Today the term Received Text or Textus Receptus is applied loosely to any text of Erasmus, Stephanus, Beza or Elzevir vintage, or even to the hybrid text that underlies the King James Version.*"

---

COMMENT #159. When Price refers to "*the hybrid text that underlies the King James Version*," I resent his terminology greatly! In over 99% of the cases, the Greek Words that underlie the King James Bible are those of Beza's 5th edition 1598. Dr. Frederick Scrivener's Greek edition indicated only 190 places where the King James translators chose a Greek Word from some other source. This is less than 0.01% of the some 140,000 Greek Words in the New Testament. How can Price consider this slight difference a "*hybrid text*"? This is a horrendous falsehood on his part.

---

# Price's Lie of Few MSS For KJB

STATEMENT #160. (p. 259) "*Even though this text is based on a relatively few manuscripts, all from only one textual tradition this 'Received Text' has acquired the status of absolute authority in some circles.*"

**COMMENT #160.** Price has outdone himself when he falsely stated that the Received Text is "*based on a relatively few manuscripts*." What a gigantic lie! When did Price go to school? How can he say that over 5,210 "*manuscripts*" is "*few*"? As of 1967, Kurt Aland of Munster, Germany, had a total of 5,255 manuscripts in copy format. According to Dr. Jack Moorman's book, *Forever Settled* (BFT #1428 @ $20.00 + $5.00 S&H), there are only a "*few*" Gnostic Critical Text manuscripts that survived (Vatican, Sinai, and only 43 others) whereas the rest of these manuscripts (5,210) were the Traditional Text variety, Price has the whole thing backwards.

As for Price's other falsehood, "*from only one textual tradition*," there are no such things as "*textual traditions*," or "*families*," or "*text-types*." As I have explained various times in this book, each manuscript, as Dean Burgon has stated, is an "*orphan*" with no relation to any other manuscript. Price has accepted Westcott and Hort's false "*genealogy*" or "*family*" of manuscripts unproven and impossible theory, sad to say. As for Price's statement that the Traditional Received Text is an "*absolute authority*," I am one who accepts it as such. The Hebrew, Aramaic, and Greek Words underlying the King James Bible I accept as the verbal, plenary, Preserved originals. Price is untrue when he talks about "*one textual tradition*." Dean Burgon has it right when he wrote:

> "*The living inhabitants of a village, congregated in the churchyard where the bodies of their forgotten progenitors for 1000 years repose without memorials of any kind,* [In other words, there are no gravestones in this cemetery.]*--is a faint image of the relation which subsists between extant copies of the Gospels and the sources from which they were derived.*" [Dean John W. Burgon, *Revision Revised*, p. 256].

# Price's Wrong KJB N.T. Greek Text

**STATEMENT #161.** (p. 261) Under the caption of "*The Text of the A.V. 1611*," Price wrote: "*The Greek New Testaments used by the translators of the King James Version of 1611 were Erasmus' texts of 1527 and 1535. Stephanus' text of 1550 and 1551, Beza's text of 1598, and the Complutensian Polyglot of 1522.*"

**COMMENT #161.** Price gives a very false impression here, as though the King James Bible translators used all four of these Greek editions on an equal basis. This is erroneous. As Dr. Scrivener has stated in the preface of *Scrivener's Annotated Greek New Testament* (BFT #1670 @ $35.00 + $5.00 S&H), this is simply not the case. In all but 190 places Beza's

5th edition of 1598 was used. The inclusion of all four of these Greek editions is misleading.

# Scrivener's Greek N.T. Text

**STATEMENT #162.** (pp. 261-262) Price wrote: *"Scrivener's edition* is now distributed by the Trinitarian Bible Society of London."

   **COMMENT #162.** *"Scrivener's edition"* is not only distributed by the Trinitarian Bible Society of London, but also by the Dean Burgon Society and the **Bible For Today** in Collingswood, New Jersey under the title: *Scrivener's Annotated Greek New Testament* (BFT #1670 @ $35.00 + $5.00 S&H). I wonder why Price did not tell his readers about this photographic reproduction of Scrivener's original New Testament. I'm sure he knows about this enlarged edition showing over 5,600 places where the Critical Text and the English Revised Version has departed from this text.

# Price's False KJB Greek Text

**STATEMENT #163.** (p. 262) Price has a chart entitled *"Textual Basis for the King James Version of 1611."*

   **COMMENT #163.** In this chart, Price does two false and erroneous things:

   (1) He falsely lists five bases for the King James Bible as though they are all equal and important enough to list. He lists *"Erasmus, Stephanus, Beza, Complutensian Polyglot, and the Latin Vulgate."* The truth of the matter is that Beza's 5th edition of 1598 bore 99.99% of the basis for the King James Bible. In no way were the other four sources listed major bases.

   (2) The second false and erroneous things in this chart is that the King James Version 1611 was the basis for *"Scrivener's Textus Receptus (1894)."* No bigger lie and falsehood could be imagined. He is stating that Scrivener's Greek text came from the King James Bible. The truth of the matter is that the King James Bible's basis in 99.99% of the time was Beza's 5th edition of 1598. Scrivener's *Greek New Testament* gave the Greek Words on which the King James was based. He did not *"back translate"* from the King James Bible to Greek as Price and others have falsely claimed without any basis in fact and proof.

# Price's False Byzantine Terminology

**STATEMENT #164.** (p. 262) Price has a false caption as *"The Textus Receptus Differs from the Byzantine Text"* He then states: *"The advocates of the Textus Receptus generally argue that it is essentially identical to the Byzantine Text."*

**COMMENT #164.** The Textus Receptus and the Byzantine or Majority Text are "*essentially identical*." If you compare the 140,521 Greek Words in the New Testament with the approximate 1,500 variations in the so-called "*Majority Text*" of either Hodges and Farstad or Robinson and Pierpont, we find a 93% agreement. This grade would be either an "A" or an "A-" in a classroom, depending on the school. I would consider these two texts "*essentially identical*." You could never say that with any two of the critical manuscripts of the Vatican, Sinai, or any of their 43 relatives. In the Gospels alone, the Vatican and Sinai differ in over 3,000 places according to Herman Hoskier's scholarly work, *Codex B and Its Allies* (BFT #1643, 924 pages @ $64.00 + $8.00 S&H).

**STATEMENT #165.** Page 263, Price is referring to Edward Hills and said: "*Here he refers to the two texts as identical...*"

**COMMENT #165.** Price used the term "*essentially identical*" on page 262, rather than merely "*identical*." There is a world of difference between these two terms. Price despises the work of Dr. Hills. Perhaps this is why he used this false overstatement here.

**STATEMENT #166.** (p. 263) "*It is true that the two texts are quite similar, but they differ in 1500 or more places, some of which differences are more than trivial.*"

**COMMENT #166.** Price is referring to Hills' stated differences between the "*Traditional Text*" (what Price refers to as either the "*Majority Text*" or the "*Byzantine Text*") and the "*Textus Receptus*." It is amusing to have Price here refer to these two texts as "*quite similar*," when he earlier disputed the words "*essentially identical*." It is also interesting also to note that Price agrees that "*some*" of these "*differences*" are "*more than trivial*."

**STATEMENT #167.** (p. 263) "*Therefore, the Textus Receptus must be regarded as a departure from the Byzantine Text, a separate tradition of its own.*"

**COMMENT #167.** This is absolutely false. The Textus Receptus is in about 93% agreement with the Traditional (or Greek, or Byzantine) Text. "1500" places out of "140,521" Greek N.T. Words (about only 7%) does not mean "*a departure from the Byzantine Text*," but, on the contrary, are "*essentially identical*" or, as Price himself agrees, occupy a "*quite similar*" relationship.

**STATEMENT #168.** (p. 264) "*This view presupposes that the Textus Receptus underlying the King James Version was providentially preserved over against all other text traditions*."

**COMMENT #168.** I am one who believes that the "*Textus Receptus underlying the King James Version*" was "*providentially preserved*" by the Lord. To put it clearly, I believe that the original Hebrew, Aramaic, and Greek Words have been "*preserved*" by God in the Words underlying the King James Bible. What's wrong with this position? Those Preserved Words are the exact, inspired, inerrant, infallible Words of the originals themselves.

# Price's "Back-Translation" Heresy

**STATEMENT #169.** (pp. 264-265) "*This particular text form did not exist in any manuscript or in any printed edition until the mid-nineteenth century when it was produced through a form of back-translation to match the English words of the King James Version*."

**COMMENT #169.** This statement by Price is pathetically false for a number of reasons.

✦(1) First, as I have stated many times, the Traditional Received Text is not by any means a "*text form*." Such "*forms*" are a figment of heretic Hort's mind in order to sell by devious lies his form of the Gnostic Critical Text of 1881.

✦(2) The second great falsehood is Price's lie that the Traditional Received Text "*did not exist in any manuscript*" until "*the mid-nineteenth century*." As I mentioned before, this Traditional Received Text is to be found in over 5,210 manuscripts, all of which pre-dated "*the mid-nineteenth century*" by many hundreds of years. Why does Price lie and try to deceive his readers in this way?

✦(3) The greatest monstrous falsehood in Price's statement is his untrue charge that the Traditional Received Text in Scrivener's edition was "*back-translation to match the English words of the King James Version.* What Price is doing here in this scandalous attack on Dr. Frederick Scrivener is to call him a liar and a deceiver because Scrivener stated very clearly that his edition was not a "*back-translation*" but an edition based upon Beza's 5th edition of 1598 with only 190 places where other sources were chosen by the King James translators. Our readers can get a photographic reproduction of Scrivener's edition by ordering from the Dean Burgon Society or from the **Bible For Today** *Scrivener's Annotated Greek New Testament* **[BFT #1670 @ $35.00 + $5.00 S&H].** You can read Scrivener's Preface for yourself as to how this edition was produced–certainly not by "*back-translation*" from

English to Greek. This false charge is a lie from the "*father*" of lies (John 8:44).

# The TR Was From the Beginning

**STATEMENT #170.** (p. 265) "*If one insists that this Textus Receptus is the flawless edition of the Greek New Testament, the very Word of God, then the church did not have a flawless copy of the Word of God for almost 2,000 years, and then only in English! Consequently, it is clear that the text of the Textus Receptus was not 'kept pure in all ages.'*"

> **COMMENT #170.** In making this statement, Price is attempting to say that the Traditional Text did not appear for "*almost 2,000 years*" in Dr. Scrivener's Greek edition. This implication is totally false. This Traditional Received Text was the original Greek Words of the New Testament writers.

My thirty-seven historic links (referred to above in **COMMENT #108** [(cf. my book, *Defending the King James Bible*, pp. 44-48 [BFT #1594 @ $12.00 + $5.00 S&H]) show that this text was from the beginning of the Apostolic age. This is in contrast to the Gnostic Critical Text of the Vatican and the Sinai manuscripts which were not even in existence until the Gnostics of Alexandria, Egypt, altered the original text in about 250 A.D. to conform to their over 356 doctrinal heresies.

**STATEMENT #171.** (p. 266) Price is speaking of most of the early leaders and theologians in Evangelicalism and Fundamentalism who accepted the principles of textual criticism. "*They accepted the textual principles, not because they lacked the discernment to see any underlying error, but because they recognized my principles to be reasonably sound and consistent with their understanding of inspiration and providential preservation. It is inappropriate to accuse those spiritual giants of being gullible.*"

**COMMENT #171.** Why is it "*inappropriate to accuse those spiritual giants of being gullible*"? Price is trying to justify early Fundamentalists and Evangelicals for their acceptance of "**textual criticism**" and the Gnostic Critical Text. He wrote: "*It is inappropriate to accuse those spiritual giants of being gullible.*" They indeed were "*gullible.*" They did not bother to examine the facts that were made crystal clear by such Bible-believing men as Dean John William Burgon in his five major books on this subject. All five of these books are available at the Dean Burgon Society, P.O. Box 347, Collingswood, New Jersey 08108, or at the **Bible For Today**, 900 Park Avenue, Collingswood, New Jersey 08108. These books can also be ordered online at either www.DeanBurgonSociety.org or also by going to www.BibleForToday.org.

> I do not in any way condone these so-called "*spiritual giants*" (including Price) who accepted the results of heretics Bishop Westcott and Professor Hort. Here is a list of Dean Burgon's five books that were available to all of those Fundamentalists and Evangelicals of the past and those of today, as well, since they are all in print in hardback books.
> 1.  *The Revision Revised* (BFT #611 @ $25.00 + $5.00 S&H)
> 2.  *The Last Twelve Verses of Mark* (BFT #1139 @ $15.00 + $5.00 S&H)
> 3.  *The Traditional Text* (BFT #1159 @ $16.00 + $5.00 S&H)
> 4.  *Causes of Corruption* (BFT #1160 @ $15.00 + $5.00 S&H)
> 5.  *Inspiration and Interpretation* (BFT #1220 @ $15.00 + $5.00 S&H)

I urge all of my readers to order at least one of these books (if not all) by Dean John W. Burgon who has completely dismantled the views of men like Westcott and Hort in times past and like Price and his current Fundamental and Evangelical friends in our present day.

# Price Questions A Preserved Text

**STATEMENT #172.** (p. 268) Price is arguing against God's preservation of His original Words of the Bible. He wrote: "*This presumption implies God's providence was active in* ***preserving the text in the era of the ancient versions****--the Septuagint, the Latin Vulgate, the Syriac, the Armenian, the Ethiopic, the Coptic, and others.*"

> **COMMENT #172.** God did preserve His Words "*preserving the text in the era of the ancient versions*," but was not compelled to preserve those "*ancient versions*" themselves, only His Hebrew, Aramaic, and Greek Words. It has nothing to do with preservation of translations.

# The Phony "Majority Text"

**STATEMENT #173.** (p. 268) "*But the plot thickens, because the manuscripts Erasmus had available to him differed often from the* **Traditional Text** *(the consensus of the majority of manuscripts)* *in more than 1500 places.*"

**COMMENT #173.** Price is dead wrong in thinking that his favorite "*Majority Text*" is the "*Traditional Text.*" His "*Majority Text*" is not "**the consensus of the majority of manuscripts**" at all. Dr. Jack Moorman carefully points out in his book, *Hodges/Farstad's Majority Text Refuted* [BFT

#1617 @ $16.00 + $7.00 S&P], that Price's so-called "*Majority Text*" is not a majority of anything. Rather, it is a reiteration of the consensus of only the 414 manuscripts that Von Soden had in his possession. 414 manuscripts (13%) is nowhere a "*majority*" (51%) of over 5,255 manuscripts as of 1967. Price's "*1500 places*" (thirteen percent) is not a "*majority*" of anything, even if all 414 manuscripts were in agreement. It is a contrived "*1500 places*," not a real one at all.

# We Don't Depend on Erasmus

**STATEMENT #174.**   (p. 269)  "*Hills presumed that God guided Erasmus, the editors, and the printers. . .*"

**COMMENT #174.**  I do not know whether "*God guided*" "*Erasmus*" in his edition of the Greek New Testament, or not. There is no proof that He did not, nor proof that He did. I believe Erasmus used the proper Greek manuscripts that conformed to the Traditional Text rather than the Gnostic Critical Text.

> But remember, the King James Bible was not based upon Erasmus' text of 1516, but on Beza's 5th edition of 1598, 82 years later.

# Price's 414 "Few" Manuscripts

**STATEMENT #175.**   (page 271)  "*Concerning such uncertainty, Hills acknowledged that Erasmus selected some readings that were supported by few or no Greek manuscripts, over against alternative readings that are supported by a consensus by the Greek witnesses.*"

**COMMENT #175.**  Price should not speak too loudly about "*few*" Greek manuscripts. His Gnostic critical Greek text is founded upon less than 1% of the manuscript evidence that has been preserved for us (45 out of 5,255). When using the phrase "*consensus by the Greek witnesses*," Price is referring to his favorite "*Majority Text*" which, as I have said before, is not a "*majority*" of anything. It was based upon a tentative text based on Von Sodden's notes. He had only 414 manuscripts (13% of the whole) in his possession, not all 5,255. How can that be a "*majority*"?

# The TR Is Not A "Single Witness"

**STATEMENT #176.**  (p. 271)  "*Even in those places where the Textus Receptus reading has support from the majority of Greek manuscripts, often the alternate reading has greater certainty because it is supported by the consensus of multiple ancient independent witnesses, whereas the Textus Receptus reading can be traced back to a single ancient witness—one late text*" *tradition."*

     **COMMENT #176.** This is such a blatant falsehood and distortion of truth that it is incomprehensible how he can get away with saying so many lies in one sentence! I cannot let him get away with such deceptions which he has foisted upon his readers.

  (1) Price's mention of "*multiple ancient independent witnesses*" is simply false. Dr. Jack Moorman has analyzed the 5,255 manuscripts available in 1967 to Kurt Aland (cf. *Forever Settled* [BFT #1428 @ $20.00 + $5.00 S&H]). He found that Price's "*multiple*" Gnostic "*ancient independent witnesses*" were merely the Vatican, the Sinai, and 43 other manuscripts. This is less than 1% of the 5,255 manuscripts available to Kurt Aland as of 1967. If Price thinks 45 manuscripts (less than 1% of the evidence) is "*multiple*," I suggest that he go back to grade school and take a course in mathematics.

  (2) *As for "the Textus Receptus reading* [being] *traced back to a single ancient witness*," again, I suggest that Price return to grade school and learn the meaning of "*a single ancient witness*." The Traditional Received Text is based on the remaining 5,210 manuscripts (over 99% of the evidence that has been preserved. How can Price call this "*single*"? He is trying to say that the over 5,000 manuscripts of the Textus Receptus are to only be counted as one witness. No, these manuscripts are all independent witnesses. These are not just one, but separate witnesses for the truth.

  (3) As for Price's calling the Traditional Received Text a "*late text tradition*," let me remind you of some things concerning whether or not this "*text tradition*" is "*late*." I have mentioned earlier *Early MSS, Church Fathers, & the Authorized Version* by Dr. Jack Moorman (BFT #3230 @ $20.00 + $5.00 S&H). In this book, Dr. Moorman repeated a similar study that had been made previously by Dean John Burgon and his associates. This has been documented in his book, *The Traditional Text* (BFT #1159 @ $16.00 + $5.00 S&H, pp. 99ff.) Dean Burgon proved that the Traditional Received Text was not "*late*" as Price falsely stated. He found, when looking at the quotations of 76 early Church Fathers who died 400 A.D. or before, that they had quoted Words that were exclusively in the Traditional Received Text in a ratio of 3 to 2 (60% to 40%) compared with the "neologian text" or critical Greek text. Dr. Moorman made a similar study (cited above) and found an even higher ratio of the Traditional Received Text in these early Church Fathers to be 70% to 30%. How can Price claim that church leaders who lived in 150, 200, and 350 A.D. are somehow "*late*"? As a matter of fact, the Traditional Received Text is the text of the original Greek New Testament.

# Price's Error On "God-Guided"

**STATEMENT #177.** (p. 272) *"But these admissions are serious blemishes in his own presumption. If God did guide Erasmus and the subsequent editors and printers then the Textus Receptus should be flawless; there should be only the one standard edition recognized by all. God is not the author of error or confusion. But since, by his own admission, the Textus Receptus still contains flaws and blemishes that remain uncorrected, and still exist in several contradictory editions, then Hills' presumption of God-guided editing and printing is subject to serious doubt and not maximum certainty."*

**COMMENT #177.** Price makes the term, *"God-guided,"* an equivalent of being *"inspired by God."* This is foolish. Hills never equated being *"led"* by God to being *"inspired by God."* As for his opinion that *"flaws and blemishes"* are in the *"Textus Receptus,"* his favorite so-called *"Majority Text"* in adopting some of the Gnostic Critical Text readings has been flawed.

# Price Trashes The Textus Receptus

**STATEMENT #178.** (p. 276) Price's caption is: *"The Textus Receptus Is Not To Be Preferred."* Then he wrote: *"After examining the textual background of the Textus Receptus and the arguments supporting it, one should conclude that it is not to be preferred over the Majority Text or the text derived by the Reasoned Eclectic method."*

**COMMENT #178.** I disagree strongly with Price's conclusions in smashing the *Textus Receptus*. I disagree strongly with Price's exaltation of the so-called *"Majority Text"* of Hodges and Farstad that differs from the *Textus Receptus* in around 1500 places. I also disagree strongly with Price's good word for the Gnostic Critical Text is so-called *"Reasoned Eclectic"* method (whatever that might be) which differs from the *Textus Receptus* in over 8,000 places.

# The "Textual Emendations" Charge

**STATEMENT #179.** (pp. 277-279) Price's Chapter 13 is entitled: *"Textual Emendations Were Made in the King James Version."* He wrote; *"These emendations cannot be justified on the basis of superior scholarly judgment of the 1611 translators because equally competent scholars are alive and well today, the knowledge of the Biblical languages is far more advanced, and textual-critical knowledge is more advanced than in the 17th Century."*

**COMMENT #179.** In the first place, I deny that there were "*Textual Emendations*" in the King James Bible. Secondly, this is the man who says he uses the King James Bible, preaches from the King James Bible and loves it.

He wrote on page xii:

"*In my early days, it never entered my mind that **the King James Version needed revision in modern English** because I cut my teeth on that edition of the Bible, memorizing it from early childhood. . . . It was not until I began teaching in seminary that I discovered I was investing a worthwhile percentage of my time teaching Elizabethan English in my classes instead of Bible*." (p. 3)

After Price gives his background with the King James Bible in his "*early childhood*," he begins to rip it apart. When he compares the "*superior scholarly judgment of the 1611 translators*" to the "*equally competent scholars*" of today, it is quite a laugh.

There is not one current "*scholar*," including Price, who can hold a candle to the scholars who gave us the King James Bible! For the details of some of the King James translators, I refer you to my book, *Defending the King James Bible*, Chapter III [BFT #1594 @ $12.00 + $5.00 S&H] on the "*Superior Translators of the King James Bible*."

As far as the "*knowledge of the Biblical languages is far more advanced*," and the other things he said, this again is folly. The King James translators had far more "*knowledge of the Biblical languages*" than any of the puffed-up self-appointed "*scholars*" today. They knew completely the Greek language, and the cognate languages of the Hebrew, the Aramaic, such as the Coptic, and the Arabic. They were also masters of the English language. That is why we have such a beautiful King James Bible.

One of the translators, for instance, was John Bois. At the age of five years he had read the Bible IN HEBREW. Think what kind of people in our day have anything even approaching the background of this man, John Bois. At age six John Bois could write Hebrew legibly and in fair and elegant character.

# Price Downs KJB Translators Skill

**STATEMENT #180.**    (p. 278) On footnote 4. Price wrote: "*Christian scholars had recently begun to study Hebrew, and the systematic study of Hebrew grammar and lexicography was in its infancy in the 17th and 18th Century.*"

**COMMENT #180.** I do not agree with this at all. The "*scholars*" who gave us the King James Bible knew their Hebrew, Aramaic, Greek, and all of the cognate or sister languages far better than Price and his other boastful "*scholars*." Again, I urge the reader to read my Chapter III of *Defending the King James Bible* [BFT #1594 @ $12.00 +$5.00 S&H] and see for yourself their scholastic ability, their knowledge of all of the languages of the Bible, and their many writings. Please don't let Price fool you on this matter.

# The Ruckman Smear Again

**STATEMENT #181.** (p. 279) In footnote #4, Price wrote: "*This topic is discussed in Chapter 13 in regard to Edward F. Hills' view of God-guided providence. Others who follow Hills' defense of the Textus Receptus accept this idea of providence. Peter Ruckman asserts that the King James Version translators were divinely inspired when they translated the AV*"

> **COMMENT #181.** In the first place, Price is again wrongly equating "*God- guided providence*" with "*divine inspiration*." As I have mentioned before, this is nonsense. In the second place, Price is deceptively and wrongly trying to yoke up Dr. Hills, and others who are close to his position, with Peter Ruckman. This is a sneaky trick indeed! I have nothing to do with the Ruckman approach and view of the King James Bible and his view that the King James Bible is "*divinely inspired*." Price is also dead wrong when he alleges that Peter Ruckman believes that "*the King James Version translators were divinely inspired*."

Though Price believes in this heresy of the original writers being "*inspired*," it is false. Price's position on this is found in **STATEMENT #44** above, Price spoke of *the words that were written by the inspired prophets and apostles*." He believes the "prophets and apostles" were "*inspired*." This is heresy! It was the Words that they wrote down that were God-breathed and "*inspired by God*," not the writers themselves.

This is not Ruckman's position. Ruckman speaks of the "*words*" of the "*translators*" as being "*inspired*," not the "*translators*" themselves. So Price has misspoken Ruckman's position here as he twists, to his shame, the positions of the anti-Ruckmanites, like myself, who have a sound position defending the King James Bible and its underlying Hebrew, Aramaic, and Greek Words.

# Price's 228 So-Called Emendations

**STATEMENT #182.** (p. 282) Price's caption is: *"Emendations Were Made in the Old Testament."* He wrote: *"Although emendations of the New Testament were few and trivial, the same cannot be said for the emendations of the Old Testament. There are at least 228 emendations to the Old Testament; some are justifiable, but many are not."*

**COMMENT #182.** What does Price mean by an *"emendation"*? In their wisdom, the King James Bible translators chose the Hebrew Word they felt was correct in all of Price's alleged *"228 emendations."* In what sense is this an *"emendation"*? Who is Price to say that any changes they may have made in the Hebrew they were usually following were *"emendations"*? If they wanted to pick another Hebrew Word that was found in another text instead of the Ben Chayyim Edition of the Hebrew, they were within their rights for doing it. With an entire Bible of almost 800,000 Words, and with an Old Testament of over 610,000 Words, what is a tiny alleged *"228 emendations"* (even if they were truly what Price says they are)?

# The KJB's Hebrew O.T. Text

**STATEMENT #183.** (p. 294) Price's caption is: *"Conclusion: The King James Version does not Follow the Traditional Hebrew Text."*

**COMMENT #183.** Price's words are totally misleading to his readers. I repeat. 228 places out of 610,000 is so minute, it is inconceivable for Price to say the King James Bible translators did not *Follow the Traditional Hebrew Text."* They certainly did follow what they considered to be the *"Traditional Hebrew Text"* as they believed it faithfully to be.

# No "Inspired" Prophets & Apostles

**STATEMENT #184.** (p. 312) Price's Chapter 14 is entitled: *"Modern English Versions are Examined."* He wrote: *"After all, the Hebrew and Greek words originally written by the divinely inspired prophets and apostles constitute the divinely inspired, inerrant, authoritative Word of God."*

**COMMENT #184.** Here again is Price's enunciation of heresy regarding Biblical inspiration. Where did he go to school to learn this heresy? Who taught him this? Or did he teach himself? He is a well-trained scholar who is able to interpret the only verse in the New Testament that speaks of *"inspiration."* The Greek Words that pertain to

> the Bible's inspiration in 2 Timothy 3:16, are three in number.   Price
> knows them very well.

They are: "*PASA GRAPHE THEOPNEUSTOS* . . ." Our King James Bible accurately renders them, "*All Scripture is given by inspiration of God.*" It says literally, "*All Scripture* (referring to the Words) *is God-breathed.*" Price should know that God breathed-out Words, not people such as "*prophets and apostles.*"

# What Is The Final Authority?

**STATEMENT #185.** (p. 313) "*Many who defend the King James Version as the final authority are concerned that the original Hebrew and Greek words of the prophets and apostles have not been preserved throughout history and are not available today.*"

**COMMENT #185.** Price is speaking of the position of Peter Ruckman and his followers who do "*defend the King James Version as the final authority.*" Though I am a strong defender of the King James Bible in our present time, I do not believe that any translation on earth, in whatever language, should ever be termed as "*final authority.*" I believe that the "*final authority*" must ever be placed in the preserved original Hebrew, Aramaic, and Greek Words underlying the King James Bible. The King James Bible, because of its accurate translation of those Words, can honestly and truly be called God's Words kept intact in English.

# Price's Weak View of Preservation

**STATEMENT #186.** (p. 313) "*But it is not as if God were unable to preserve the original Hebrew and Greek words–the words are preserved by a consensus of the surviving manuscripts and other witnesses. It is not a matter of preservation, but of being able to discern which of the preserved words are the original ones.*"

**COMMENT #186.** When he says that "*the words are preserved by a consensus of the surviving manuscripts and other witnesses,*" Price really doesn't know where the "*preserved*" Words of God are. I (and the **Bible For Today** and the Dean Burgon Society) believe that the "*Preserved*" original Words are in a specific document. It is the Hebrew, Aramaic and Greek Words that underlie our King James Bible. We are not at sea as far as where the Words are. We have them nailed down. This is a matter of faith, I realize, but it is also a matter of fact. There are many manuscripts (over 5,210 or over 99% of the surviving evidence) that give solid evidence in favor of the Textus Receptus against the very few manuscripts (45 or less than 1%) in favor of the Critical Texts of either the Westcott and Hort, the United Bible Societies, or the Nestle/Aland. We don't have to go all over the world to find the Words of God. God promised to *"**preserve**"* His Words for us, and I believe He has done this in the Hebrew, Aramaic and Greek Words underlying our King James Bible.

**STATEMENT #187.**   (p. 315) Price's Chapter 15 is entitled: *"Modern Versions Support **Orthodox Doctrine**."* He quoted me in disdain: *"All three of these: [NKJV, NASV, and NIV], to a lesser or greater extent have all used perversion, paraphrase, and dynamic equivalency. And we believe there are three ways this has been done. They have added to the words of God; subtracted from the words of God; and they have changed the words of God; and **we believe they are theologically in error, as well**."*

**COMMENT #187.**   Price thinks that only *"**orthodox** doctrine"* is included in these versions. The *"NKJV"* refers to the footnotes that are found in the study edition.

I stand by the statement that *"**we believe they are theologically in error, as well**."* Price is drastically wrong in his denial of doctrinal errors in the modern versions. I refer once again to pages 119-312 in Dr. Jack Moorman's book, *Early Manuscripts, Church Fathers, and the Authorized Version* [BFT #3230 @ $20.00 + $5.00 S&H] for a listing of over 356 doctrinal passages in the Gnostic Critical Text which are not doctrinally *"orthodox."* There are some *"orthodox"* doctrines in the Gnostic Critical Text because the Gnostics from Alexandria, Egypt, who altered the Vatican and Sinai manuscripts could not get their hands on all the many Greek New Testament manuscripts. They couldn't take away all of the orthodox doctrines, but they did pervert over 356 doctrinal passages.

# Price Weak On 1 Timothy 3:16

**STATEMENT #188.** (p. 322) Under the caption of *"1 Timothy 3:16,"* Price quoted the King James Bible as *"**God** was manifest in the flesh."* Then he wrote: *"However, some ancient Greek manuscripts have a pronoun where **the Textus Receptus has the word God**."*

**COMMENT #188.**   Yes, *"**the Textus Receptus has the word God**"* in this verse. The Gnostic heretics who changed the Critical Texts of the Vatican and Sinai manuscripts did not believe in the deity of the Lord Jesus Christ nor did they believe He was *"**manifest in the flesh**."* For this reason, they removed *"**God**"* from their text. The modern versions like the NASV, NIV, ESV, RSV, NRSV and others (with the exception of the New King James Version) also omit "*God.*" This removal is a serious doctrinal heresy that Price's fancy word-play cannot refute.

# Price Praises New Version's Doctrines

**STATEMENT #189.** (p. 382) Part Eight is called: "*Criticism of the Versions is Faulty.*" Price wrote: "*Those who criticize the modern versions choose an isolated verse that fails to support a doctrine as explicitly as the King James Version, accusing the versions of denying the doctrine. In a Bible version having many passages that strongly support a doctrine, lack of support in one passage does not constitute denial.*"

**COMMENT #189.** When Price wrote: "*lack of support in one passage does not constitute denial.*" what kind of answer is that? It is certainly a "*denial*" of that doctrine in that passage. As I have said before, the Gnostic heretics who perverted the Vatican and Sinai manuscripts did not have <u>all</u> the manuscripts. I am thankful for that. Thus they could not pervert <u>all</u> the New Testament. But when they deny doctrine in over 356 passages, they are not to be trusted at all. In 1 Timothy 3:16, for instance, can you tell me where else in God's Word you can find any statement that is as specific as "*God was manifest in the flesh*"? Philippians Chapter 2 has a reference, but it is not as specific as God being manifest in the flesh.

Here is another example where doctrines have been removed from Price's text. When the Lord Jesus Christ is made a liar in John Chapter 7, "*I go not up YET to the feast,*" the modern versions take out the word "*YET*" as does the Critical Greek text that underlies this verse. That makes Jesus a liar. This is never justified in any other verse in the new versions. These are not found in any other place as Price has said. The wording in the Gnostic Critical Text in Luke 2:22 implies (by changing "*her*" to "*their*") that the Lord Jesus Christ was a sinner Who needed to be "cleansed." This is serious heresy that, apparently, Price is content with.

# Price Praises the NIV Doctrinally

**STATEMENT #190.** (p. 383) Price wrote: "*In either case the wording of the NIV constitutes a meaningful and doctrinally correct statement.*"

**COMMENT #190.** The NIV wording in 1 Timothy 3:16 is "*HE appeared in a body.*" But where is the solid doctrinal clause, "*God was manifest in the flesh*"? How can Price say that "*the wording of the NIV*" *constitutes a meaningful and doctrinally correct statement*"? Where is his theological compass? All of us have "appeared in a body." That is a million times different from "*GOD was manifest in the flesh*."

Dean John W. Burgon has defended "God" (THEOS) in his book, The Revision Revised (BFT #611 @ $25.00 + $5.00 S&H). The strong evidence is found on the 77 pages of 424-501. Of the manuscripts and Church Fathers having or referring to 1 Timothy 3:16, here is the score: 312 had THEOS; 8 had HO (which); 7 had HOS (who). THEOS is overwhelmingly the Word God has preserved.

# NIV's Heresies In Micah 5:2

**STATEMENT #191.** (p. 384) Price justifies the blasphemous reading of the NIV's wording of Micah 5:2 which reads: ""*But you, Bethlehem Ephrathah, though you are small among the clans of Judah, out of you will come for me one who will be ruler over Israel, whose **origins** are from of old, from ancient times*."

**COMMENT #191.** The King James Bible accurately renders Micah 5:2 as follows: "*But thou, Bethlehem Ephratah, though thou be little among the thousands of Judah, yet out of thee shall he come forth unto me that is to be ruler in Israel; whose **goings forth** have been from of old, from everlasting*."

This is a prophecy of the first coming of the Lord Jesus Christ. There are two doctrinal errors that Price does not want to call major heresies: (1) The Lord Jesus Christ did not have "*origins*." He was from everlasting in eternity past. (2) He was not merely "*from ancient times*," but "*from everlasting.*" If Price is a Fundamentalist Christian and cannot discern the NIV's heretical translation here, something is drastically deficient in his Biblical theology.

# Modern Versions Doctrinal Errors

**STATEMENT #192.** (p. 386) Price wrote: "*The **modern versions** are also rejected because of **alleged errors in them**, for example, in Mark 1:2 the King James Version reads 'As it is written **in the prophets**,' whereas most modern versions read, 'As it is written **in Isaiah** the prophet.' The expression introduces a mixed quotation derived from both Malachi and Isaiah. Consequently, the **modern versions** are believed to contain an error because the quotation is not just from Isaiah while the King James Version is viewed as correct because it refers to 'prophets.'*"

**COMMENT #192.** (p. 386) It is more than mere "*alleged errors*" contained in "*modern version*." The "*errors*" are real and genuine. Here is the portion of the Old Testament which is quoted in Mark 1:2: It is found in Malachi 3:1: "*Behold, I will send my messenger, and he shall prepare the way before me:*" With all of Price's trying to cop out of this being an "*error*," he has not quoted the verse in the book of "*Isaiah*" from which this erroneous and faulty Gnostic Critical Text is taken. If Price were to look in any concordance for the words, "*I will send my messenger*" or "*He shall prepare the way*," he cannot find either of these phrases (which are the heart of Mark 1:2) in any verse of Isaiah or in any verse in any other reference than Malachi 3:1. The King James Bible's Traditional Received Text's wording "*in the prophets*" is correct and "*in the prophet Isaiah*" is incorrect.

As for the phrase "*in the prophets*," this is the phrase used to indicate one of the three sections of the Hebrew Old Testament as is mentioned in Luke 24:44: "*And he said unto them, These are the words which I spake unto you, while I was yet with you, that all things must be fulfilled, which were written in the law of Moses, and in the prophets, and in the psalms, concerning me.*"

# The Versions' Error in Luke 2:22

**STATEMENT #193.** (p. 387) "*In Luke 2:22 the modern versions read the days of their purification. The King James Version reads the days of her purification. The modern versions are accused of factual error because the purification rite was limited to the mother (Leviticus 12:1-8).*"

**COMMENT #193.** That is correct, the "*purification*" is limited to the mother, not the father and not the baby. The Gnostic Critical Text reading of "*their purification*" is in both factual and doctrinal error.

(1) Not only is "*their purification*" not "*according to the Law of Moses*," as Luke 2:22 clearly declares;

(2) but also, it makes the Lord Jesus Christ out to be a sinner Who had to be "*cleansed*." This is serious doctrinal heresy! He was not a sinner, He was holy and sinless.

# Price's View of Bible Preservation

**STATEMENT #194.** (p. 389) Price's section title is: *"Modern Versions Allegedly Correct the Word of God"* Price wrote: *"Those sacred words have not been lost, but have been providentially preserved in the hundreds of surviving manuscripts (ancient Bibles), in the ancient translations, and in the quotations the Church Fathers made of biblical passages."*

---

**COMMENT #194.** Price does not know where the sacred Words are. He believes they are all over in different locations. Price, who favors the Gnostic Critical Text, lies when he talks about God's *"sacred words"* are *"preserved in the hundreds of surviving manuscripts."*

---

These Gnostic critical *"manuscripts"* have only *"survived"* in only about 45 *"manuscripts"*–Vatican, Sinai, and 43 others. Here Price's math is wrong again; 45 does not add up to *"hundreds."* The number of manuscripts *"surviving"* for the Traditional Received text are over 5,210. Many of the *"ancient translations"* also testify for the Traditional Received Text. So do the *quotations the Church Fathers made of biblical passages"* testify in 60% to 70% of the places to the Traditional Received Text.

# Truth Doesn't Need "Balance"

**STATEMENT #195.** (p. 390) Price's heading is: *"A Balanced View is Necessary."* He wrote: *"When a Bible student occasionally finds an apparent contradiction between two versions, he should not jump to the conclusion that one or the other is necessarily 'incorrect.' It is wrong to interpret a passage in isolation. Moreover, a reasonable explanation usually exists for such problems. No translation of the Bible is flawless in every detail because it is the product of finite and fallible men."*

---

**COMMENT #195.** I disagree with Price here. If the King James Bible says one thing and one of the false Gnostic Critical Text-based modern versions says another, go with the King James Bible. I take the reliable and trustworthy Traditional Received Greek text that underlies the King James Bible. I agree with Price when he said: *"a reasonable explanation usually exists for such problems."* The "explanation" is that the modern versions are based on the wrong Greek text and the King James Bible is based on the right Greek text and should be followed. I don't try to *"balance"* truth with error. I take the truth and reject error.

# Don't Trust "Modern Versions"

**STATEMENT #196.** (p. 390) Price's heading is: *"Modern Versions Help a Person Understand the King James Version."* He wrote: *"Many conservative Christians have chosen to continue using the KJV of 1769 rather than one of the modern versions. A thoughtful choice should not be criticized; yet, vocal antagonists of __modern versions__ should not hinder a student of the Bible from __using the help of these versions__."*

**COMMENT #196.** Price talks favorably about the *"__modern versions__"* and *"__using the help of these versions__."* If you are seeking the truth of what God said in His Preserved Words of Hebrew, Aramaic, and Greek, modern versions are far more likely to hinder, confuse, and lead you astray rather than *"__help__"* you. The *"__modern versions__"* are based on inferior Hebrew, Aramaic, and Greek texts, have inferior translators, use inferior translation techniques, and have inferior theology in many places. All four of these inferior areas hinder sincere Bible students. They do not *"__help__"* them.

# Is Poetical Form Worth Errors?

**STATEMENT #197.** (p. 393) Price's heading is: *"Recognizing Poetry."* He wrote: *"While the KJV does not distinguish poetry from prose in the format of its text, modern versions clearly distinguish the two. Poetry is set forth in poetic structure, displaying the individual poetic lines and marking the strophic divisions."*

**COMMENT #197.** Rather than seeking poetry with inferior translation, you should be seeking accuracy in translation such as we have in the King James Bible versus the woeful inaccuracy of the *"__modern versions__."* Getting poetry in a particular format is no excuse for using an inaccurate paraphrase in many places.

# The KJB Is Easier To Read

**STATEMENT #198.** (p. 394) *"Moreover, many pastors and teachers of the Word in fundamental circles, refusing to be influenced by vocal peer pressure, have begun to recognize the importance of __a version that congregations can easily read__, without stumbling over archaic words and obscure word order."*

**COMMENT #198.** There is *"__a version that congregations can easily read__."* It is called *The Defined King James Bible*, published by the **Bible For Today**, 900 Park Avenue, Collingswood, New Jersey 08108. Or, it can be ordered online at **www.BibleForToday.org** as well. Uncommon words are defined accurately in the footnotes. Why can't "*congregations*" read the King James Bible? As far as being "*easily read*," the King James Bible is easier to read in most areas when compared to six other modern versions. To see the proof of this, get *The Readability of the Authorized Version* (BFT #2671 @ $6.00 + $3.00 S&H) by D. A. Waite, Jr. It is an accurate and balanced, detailed computer proof of this.

# No Modern Conservative Versions

**STATEMENT #199.** (p. 394) "*The goal of modern conservative versions is clarity with understanding, not subversive watering down of the fundamental doctrines of Scripture. The clarity of modern versions yields understanding that will aid lay people and pastors alike as they 'grow in the grace and knowledge of our Lord and Saviour Jesus Christ (2 Peter 3:18).*"

**COMMENT #199.** Where are these "*modern conservative versions*" that Price is mentioning here? With the exception of most of the Greek Words underlying the New King James Version, every other "*modern*" version is anything but "*conservative*" as to its textual base. On the contrary, they follow the Gnostic critical Greek text which is anything but "*conservative*." This applies to the New American Standard Version (NASV), the New International Version (NIV), and the more recent English Standard Version (ESV).

Using this Gnostic critical Greek text is indeed a "*subversive watering down of the fundamental doctrines of Scripture.*" Every one of the 356 doctrinal passages found in the Gnostic critical Greek text is found in one or more of the Gnostic heretics from Alexandria, Egypt, who perverted the Traditional Received Text. The above, so-called by Price as "conservative versions," use this Gnostic critical Greek text despite repeated warnings by me and many others that serious "*fundamental doctrines of Scripture*" have been compromised. These more than 356 doctrinal passages are to be found on pages 119-312 of Dr. Jack Moorman's excellent book, *Early MSS, Church Fathers, & the Authorized Version* (BFT #3230 for a gift of $20.00 + $5.00 S&H.) Price talks about the "*clarity of modern versions.*" Even if, for the sake of argument, these "*modern versions*" might have a little "*clarity*," What good is "*clarity*" if you have to sacrifice accuracy?

Over 8,000 differences exist between the Gnostic critical Greek text and the Traditional Received Text underlying the King James Bible. Though some of these differences are minor, they represent over 8,000 inaccuracies in the "*modern versions*," regardless of any alleged "*clarity*" they might contain. Reading these "modern versions" will lead you astray from getting true "*knowledge of our Lord and Saviour Jesus Christ*" in both His Person and His Work. This is <u>unforgivable.</u>

# 225 of His Statements and My Comments-- Statements ##201-225

## Stay Away From Modern Versions

**STATEMENT #200.** (p. 394) *"Even though one may not choose to adopt a modern version as an official text, <u>comparative use of conservative modern versions</u> should be an <u>integral part of every Christian's personal Bible study</u>."*

**COMMENT #200.** This is a ridiculous suggestion. Why would anyone in their right mind want to use one of what Price calls *"<u>conservative modern versions</u>"* such as the NASV, the NIV, or the ESV.

All of these so-called *"<u>conservative modern versions</u>"* use the Gnostic Critical Text in their New Testaments. All of them have inaccuracy in text, translators, translation technique, and theology. Why would anyone want to use these for *"<u>comparative use</u>"* (or any other use), when they can use the King James Bible with which accuracy in text, translators, translation technique, and theology?

We should never seek information from error when we have truth. You should get a *Defined King James Bible* to better understand uncommon words rather than turning to the dangerous, inaccurate and heresy-laden *"<u>modern versions</u>"* as a part of your *"<u>personal Bible study</u>."*

## Price Has "Uncertainty"

**STATEMENT #201.** (p. 395) Price's Chapter 16 is called: *"<u>Textual Uncertainty</u> is Insignificant."* He wrote: *"<u>Uncertainty plagues everyone</u> to some degree."*

**COMMENT #201.** *"Uncertainty"* does not *"plague"* me.

I have arrived at *"certainty"* regarding my belief in the verbal, plenary Preservation of the original inspired, inerrant, infallible Hebrew, Aramaic, and Greek Words that underlie the King James Bible. I also have a *"certainty"* about the true and faithful accuracy of the King James Bible itself.

That *"certainty"* cannot be communicated to others who don't wish to share it. From 1970 to the present, I have examined many books and documents on this subject and in this way I have arrived at my own *"certainty"* on these matters.

# TR Manuscripts Very Close

**STATEMENT #202.** (p. 395) *"It is also true that there are those who are disturbed by the uncertainty associated with the Bible, especially when they learn that biblical manuscripts do not have exactly the same words, or that various translations seem to convey different messages."*

**COMMENT #202.** It is true that *"biblical manuscripts"* do not have *"exactly the same words."* The Gnostic Vatican, Sinai, and the 43 other *"biblical manuscripts"* that agree with them have, in over 8,000 instances, different words from the Traditional Received Words underly-ing the King James Bible. In fact, these Gnostic manuscripts vary greatly from one another, as Dean Burgon has pointed out."

Singular to relate, the first, second, fourth, and fifth of these codices (B Aleph C D), but especially B and Aleph, have within the last twenty years established a tyrannical ascendency over the imagination of the Critics, which can only be fitly spoken of as a blind superstition. It matters nothing that all four are discovered, on careful scrutiny, to differ essentially, not only from ninety-nine out of a hundred of the whole body of extant MSS. besides, but even from one another. [Dean John W. Burgon, *Revision Revised*, pp. 11-12]

Herman Hoskier's research called, *Codex B and Its Allies* [BFT #1643 @ $46.00 + $8.00 S&H]) has demonstrated that B & Aleph, in the Gospels alone, differ in over 3,000 critical places. The Traditional Received Text is made up of manuscripts that differ slightly (to show that they are not carbon copies), but they are almost virtually identical as far as their words are concerned. We don't have to have *"textual uncertainty"* as Price has and many of his followers have.

**STATEMENT #203.** (p. 396) *"The fact that <u>uncertainty exists</u> about which preserved variant readings are autographic <u>does not deny the preservation or the authority of the autographic text</u>."*

**COMMENT #203.** I believe it does *"<u>deny the preservation or the authority of the autographic text.</u>"*. If *"<u>uncertainty exists</u>"* about the present New Testament Greek copies, I believe this *"<u>denies the preservation or the authority of the autographic text.</u>"*

> If a person believes the copies are defective, how do they know the originals were perfect and authoritative? Price dismisses the drastic results of *"<u>uncertainty</u>."* I have no *"<u>uncertainty</u>"* because I am certain about both the verbal plenary inspiration of the autographs, and the verbal plenary Preservation of those autographs which, I believe, underlie the King James Bible.

# Dispute Over "Final Authority"

**STATEMENT #204.** (p. 396) Price's caption is: *"The Large Number of Variants Is Insignificant in the Big Picture"* He wrote: *"The number of variant readings in the manuscripts of the Greek New Testament has caused some people to believe that an English version of the Bible has to be the <u>final authority</u> for <u>faith and practice</u> rather than the Hebrew or Greek texts."*

> **COMMENT #204.** The Preserved original Hebrew, Aramaic, and Greek Words that underlie the King James Bible must be the *"<u>final authority</u>"* for *"<u>faith and practice</u>"* rather than any translation of those original Preserved Words.

# Price's Heresy of Pushing Thoughts

**STATEMENT #205.** (p. 402) *"One of the readings is original, but even if the word were not in the autographic text, <u>the thought is implied</u> in the context--the normal expectation is that evil reports would be false."*

> **COMMENT #205.** In saying *"<u>the thought is implied</u>,"* Price is dealing with a very dangerous heresy. No one should have either a Greek word or a translation word that is merely *"<u>implied</u>."* This is never to be done. It is guesswork, hypothesis, and, as Dean Burgon would say, it is.
>
> *"<u>an excursion into cloud-land: a dream and nothing more</u>."*
> [*Revision Revised*, p. 397, see also, pp. xxvii and 251].

> The Bible is made up of Words. It is these Words that should be translated, not any "*implied*" word or "*thought*."

# Sound Doctrine Is Compromised

**STATEMENT #206.** (p. 403) "*Doctrinally, the certainty is even stronger. A few years ago, **Dennis Wisdom**, then professor of Greek at Tennessee Temple University, reported that he had just finished examining every place of variation of the Nestle/Aland Greek New Testament. He stated that no reading had any significant effect on sound doctrine unless perhaps the variant in John 5:4 might slightly affect the doctrine of angels.*"

**COMMENT #206.** What a preposterous and lying false statement of "***Dennis Wisdom***" as quoted by Price! Price is referring to a "***professor of Greek*** "who, unfortunately, has done slipshod and shoddy research. One of two things is true:

(1) either he does not know what "***sound doctrine***" is, or

(2) he did not examine "***every place of variation***."

> For the edification of both Wisdom and Price, let me urge them to provide themselves with two books and to study carefully the specific doctrinal passages where "*sound doctrine*" is absent: (1) *Early Manuscripts, Church Fathers, and the Authorized Version*, pages 119-312 [BFT #3230 @ $20.00 + $5.00 S&H] by Dr. Jack Moorman. He cites over 356 doctrinal passages together with the manuscript evidence where "*sound doctrine*" is sacrificed. (2) *Defending the King James Bible*, Chapter V, where I detail 158 of these 356 doctrinal passages and explain the doctrinal error.

# Doctrinal Irregularity Is Present

**STATEMENT #207.** (p. 403) In footnote #10, Price wrote: "*The enemies of the Critical Text (and of modern translations based on it) delight in pointing out departures from King James wording in which they infer some alleged doctrinal irregularity. Under careful scrutiny these instances turn out to be matters of private interpretation rather than sound exposition.*"

**COMMENT #207.** I am pleased to be one of Price's "***enemies of the Critical Text (and of modern translations based on it)***. It is not "***departures from King James wording***" that bother me as much as the Gnostic heretical Critical Text that is followed by these "***modern translations***" which leads them into over 356 doctrinal errors.

The "*departures from King James wording*" are often a red flag of warning that doctrinal error underlies it. The renderings in the Gnostic Critical Text versions such as the NASV, the NIV, or the ESV, for example, in verses such as John 6:47, Philippians 4:13, and 1 Timothy 3:16 illustrate such red flags.

# TR Data Are Available

**STATEMENT #208.** (p. 403) In footnote #11, Price wrote: "*I use the Traditional Text rather than the Textus Receptus because the data for the Textus Receptus are not available. The Textus Receptus is not identical with the Traditional Text, but the overall difference to the readers will be minimal.*"

**COMMENT #208.** Contrary to Price's statement, I believe that "*the data for the Textus Receptus*" are available.

The Greek New Testament Words that have been "*received by all*" are found in a number of Greek editions, the most accurate of which has been reproduced by Dr. Frederick Scrivener taken from Beza's 5ᵗʰ edition of 1598.

This text is available from **The Bible For Today**, 900 Park Avenue, Collingswood, New Jersey 08108 either in the smaller text only edition of the Trinitarian Bible Society (**BFT #471 @ $13.00 + $5.00 S&H**) or by the larger text with all of Scrivener's added features and appendix published by the Dean Burgon Society, Box 354, Collingswood, New Jersey 08108 (**BFT #1670 @ $35.00 + $5.00 S&H**). As for the name of this historic text, remember what Dean John Burgon wrote about it:

"*XIII. The one great Fact, which especially troubles him and his joint Editor,–(as well it may)--is The Traditional Greek Text of the New Testament Scriptures. Call this Text Erasmian or Complutensian,--the Text of Stephens, or of Beza, or of the Elzevirs,--call it the 'Received,' or the Traditional Greek Text, or whatever other name you please;--the fact remains, that a Text has. come down to us which is attested by a general consensus of ancient Copies, ancient Fathers, ancient Versions.*" (Dean John W. Burgon, *The Revision Revised*, p. 269).

I call it both the Traditional and the Received Text, as Dean Burgon did in this quotation. It is the text that Price abhors and seeks to destroy.

# No Uncertainty In Bible Exegesis

**STATEMENT #209.** (p. 405) *"Uncertainty exists in the Exegesis of the English Bible"*

**COMMENT #209.** Price can't get enough *"Uncertainty"* it seems. He sees it everywhere. It seems like it is like his middle name. I certainly would not want to be one of his students and go out into this world with *"uncertainty"* painted on my forehead and in my voice as I tried to preach faithfully the Words of God. I have certainty in my verse by verse *"Exegesis"* of the Words of God each Sunday.

> I was taught the *"uncertainty"* by use of the Westcott and Hort Gnostic critical Greek text at Dallas Theological Seminary from 1948 through 1953. I was not told there was any other New Testament Greek text in existence. Then about twenty years later, I was pointed to some research and sound books that convinced me I was on the wrong path. I changed to the Traditional Received Text and have had that *"certainty"* ever since.

# Modern Versions=False Doctrines

**STATEMENT #210.** (p. 415) Price's heading is: *"Uncertainty Exists in Interpretation"* He wrote: *"**Doctrinal differences do not hinge on variant readings**, because doctrine is based on passages with no textual uncertainty. **Doctrinal differences** are **not caused by the use of modern versions**, because nearly all doctrinal differences among denominations were established long before modern versions came on the scene."*

**COMMENT #210.** It is totally off-the-wall-ridiculous for Price to say that *"**doctrinal differences do not hinge on variant readings**."* Throughout my book I have shown that doctrinal differences that do hinge on variant readings. Let me repeat the previous sources where the reader can see 356 *"doctrinal differences"* and 158 of the more prominent ones:

(1) *Early Manuscripts, Church Fathers, and the Authorized Version*, pages 119-312 [**BFT #3230 @ $20.00 + $5.00 S&H**] by Dr. Jack Moorman.

> He cites over **356 doctrinal passages** together with the manuscript evidence where "**sound doctrine**" is sacrificed.

(2) *Defending the King James Bible*, Chapter V, where I detail **158 of these 356 doctrinal passages** and explain the doctrinal error.[From **COMMENT #206** above]

It is clearly false to say that these *"**doctrinal differences**"* are *"**not caused by**"* *the use of modern versions.*" These false "**versions**" have all the false doctrines that the underlying false Gnostic Greek texts have.

## Price's Uncertainty Again

**STATEMENT #211.** (p. 415) Price's heading is: "*Uncertainty is the Occasion for Faith not Doubt.*" He wrote: "*The Bible, like all other things in life has a measure of uncertainty associated with the identity, the exposition, the interpretation and the meaning of its text. Sound reason is shown that this uncertainty provides no practical basis for doubting the authenticity or authority of Scripture; . . .*"

**COMMENT #211.** Price is wrong when he proclaims: "*uncertainty provides no practical basis for doubting.*" This is the very thing Thomas the doubter had—"*uncertainty*" as to the bodily resurrection of the Lord Jesus Christ. "*Uncertainty*" is not what we have in the Bible. Price is preaching "*doubt.*"

---

Price is a modern day doubting Thomas always talking about "*uncertainty.*" Who would want to follow him as a teacher? What sort of nonsense is this? When I proclaim the Scriptures to the people of the Bible For Today Baptist Church I have certainty. Unlike Price, I have no doubt when I preach the Words of God.

---

That is what Paul told Timothy, "*Preach the word; be instant in season, out of season; reprove, rebuke, exhort with all long suffering and doctrine*" (2 Timothy 4:2). Paul didn't say one thing about preaching with "*uncertainty*" because you don't know what you are preaching is true. I'd hate to be under the preaching and teaching of Price with "*uncertainty*" coming out of his mind, his mouth, and his heart. I don't have "*uncertainty*" when it comes to the Words of God.

## Price For KJB + Modern Versions

**STATEMENT #212.** (p. 416) "*I also plan to continue to use my King James Versions and other modern versions, to employ what seems to be the best method of textual criticism, and to retain my confidence in the Hebrew*

*and Greek texts of the Bible as the divinely inspired, infallible, inerrant authoritative Word of God, in spite of occasional uncertainty.*"

**COMMENT #212.** "Uncertainty, uncertainty, uncertainty and more uncertainty" is his theme. Price said he was going "*to continue to use my King James Versions.*" Why would he want to use something he has been condemning throughout his book? He has said the Old

Testament Hebrew text is wrong, the New Testament Greek text is wrong, and the King James Bible itself is wrong. To me, it is the height of hypocrisy to affirm that he will continue to use the "*__King James Versions__*" (I guess he has a number of different ones) as well as "*__other modern versions__*." Of course, hypocrisy or not, Price is perfectly free to do what he wishes and to use whatever please him, especially in his sad state of "*__uncertainty__*." The lamentable part about it is that he has passed on to his many students he has taught through the years the disease of "*__uncertainty__*."

# Price Lies Again About TR's Origin

**STATEMENT #213.** (p. 417) Price's Chapter 17 is: "*Conclusion: Use Versions with Discernment.*" He wrote: "*In addition, the Greek text that underlies the English words of the King James Version, now known as the Textus Receptus, is a hybrid, eclectic text derived from a variety of differing earlier printed editions. __The Textus Receptus has no tangible existence until the mid-1800's when it was created__ to provide the Greek basis for the English words for the King James Version. The exact sequence of words in the Textus Receptus is not found in any known manuscript or prior printed edition.*"

**COMMENT #213.** Price is very deceitful in his description of the "*__Textus Receptus__*." As a Traditional Received Text, it goes back to the apostolic times and to its original writers. Certainly, there are small variations in its wording through the years, but it has a history and a continuity from that time to the present. As I have said before, there are 37 verifiable historical links in the history of the Traditional Received Text. [See my *Defending the King James Bible*, pp.44-48 (**BFT #1594 @ $12.00 + $5.00 S&H**).

> By his own admission, Price himself has stated above:
>
> "*The Greek New Testaments used by the translators of the King James Version of 1611 were Erasmus' texts of 1527 and 1535. Stephanus' text of 1550 and 1551, Beza's text of 1598, and the Complutensian Polyglot of 1522.*" [p. 261, above under **STATEMENT #161**]

These were the forerunners of the present Traditional Received Text or Textus Receptus. Where does Price get the "*__mid-1800's__*"? Where does he get the "*__no tangible existence__*" falsehood? Every one of the dates above are in the 1500's, not the "*__mid-1800's__*" at all. The Elzevir edition of 1613 could also be added to the "*__Received Text__*" pedigree. Let me repeat what I have quoted earlier as to the history of the Traditional Received Text from Dean John W. Burgon:

*XIII. The one great Fact, which especially troubles him and his joint Editor,--(as well it may)--is The Traditional Greek Text of the New Testament Scriptures. Call this Text Erasmian or Complutensian,-- the Text of Stephens, or of Beza, or of the Elzevirs,--__call it the-'Received,' or the Traditional Greek Text, or whatever other name you please;__--the fact remains, that a Text has come down to us which is attested by a general consensus of ancient Copies, ancient Fathers, ancient Versions."* (Dean John W. Burgon, *The Revision Revised*, p. 269).

---
**Price is seeking to rob his readers from the truth of the continuity of the Traditional Received Text.**

---

Perhaps the most serious of Price's many falsehoods in this quotation is his phrase, "__when it was created__." He is implying that the Words on which the New Testament of the King James Bible is based were "*created*" rather than formed from previous New Testament Greek editions.   In three previous **STATEMENTS (##19, 116, and 169)** above, Price has used the term "__back-translated__" or "__back-translation__" to refer to the edition of Dr. Frederick Scrivener.  He is implying the same thing here.  In truth, as Scrivener himself testifies in his Preface, his Greek text was that of Beza's 5th edition of 1598 for over 99% of it with the use of 10 other sources in about 190 places out of the over 140,000 Greek Words in the New Testament. This was truly an "*edition*," not a "*creation.*"  Price implies that Scrivener made up his Greek text himself and even translated the whole Greek text from the English King James Bible. Such nonsense, which is perpetrated by Price, not only manifests deceit and idiocy, but is also void of any documentation.  It is beneath Price's genuine scholarship, dignity and erudition.

# TR Was From The Beginning

**STATEMENT #214.** (p. 417) *"Although the Textus Receptus is a __derivative of the Byzantine text__, the text used by the Greek-speaking Orthodox Church, it differs from that text in over 1,500 places."*

---
**COMMENT #214.**  The Textus Receptus is not a "__derivative of the Byzantine text__," or any other text.  It is an independent Traditional Received Text that has descended from the originals that were written in apostolic times.

---

Price is trying to make the Textus Receptus a minor off-shoot of his favorite "__Majority Text__" which is not a majority of anything but about 414 Greek New Testament manuscripts.  I refer you again to Dean Burgon's quotation from his *Revision Revised* (page 269) referred to above in

## STATEMENT #213.

> Notice that Dean Burgon did not use either of Price's favorite terms, *"Majority Text,"* or *"Byzantine Text."* These are terms used by those who, like Price, despise the Traditional Received Text and seek to peddle either the Gnostic Critical Text or the so-called *"Byzantine or Majority Text."*

I prefer the terms used by Dean Burgon to describe the fact: *"that a Text has. come down to us which is attested by a general consensus of ancient Copies, ancient Fathers, ancient Versions."* (Dean John W. Burgon, *The Revision Revised*, p. 269).

# Eclectic Theory Is Not Eclectic

**STATEMENT #215.** (p. 418) *"Of the three major theories of textual recovery--the reasoned eclectic theory, the majority text (Byzantine) theory, and the Textus Receptus theory–the first seems to be the most reliable, contributing the least degree of uncertainty. This is true because the reasoned eclectic method takes all the evidence into account."*

**COMMENT #215.** This is another one of Price's monstrous misstatements when he wrote: *"the reasoned eclectic method takes all the evidence into account."* How can this well-educated man spew out such falsehood! The truth of the matter is that this method does not take *"all the evidence into account."* The only *"evidence"* taken *"into account"*--from Westcott and Hort to Nestle/Aland and the United Bible Societies--is the less than 1% of the surviving manuscript evidence (Vatican, Sinai, and about 43 other manuscripts). Most of the rest of the more than 99% of the evidence (over 5,210 manuscripts) the users of this so-called *"eclectic"* method do not even bother to look into. These men consider these manuscripts to be just one witness rather than 5,210 independent witnesses from all over the then-known world. If you don't believe their method is not truly *"eclectic,"* just examine what they have done with Mark 16:9-20, the last twelve verses of Mark's gospel.

> Here is the manuscript evidence in Dean Burgon's day for and against these twelve verses. The page references are from Dean Burgon's book, *The Last Twelve Verses of Mark* (BFT #1139 @ $15.00 + $5.00 S&H)
>
> a. AGAINST Mark 16:9-20:
>> (1) Codex "B" (Vatican) [p. 70]
>> (2) Codex "Aleph" (Sinai) [p. 70]
>
> b. FOR Mark 16:9-20:
>> (1) 18 Uncials [p. 71]

> (2) c. 600 Cursive Copies [p. 71]
>
> (3) Every known Uncial or Cursive
>       in existence!  (except Vatican & Sinai) [p.71]
>
> (4) Every known Lectionary of the
>       East! [p. 210]

So much for Price's lie that "*the reasoned eclectic method takes all the evidence into account*." No matter how Price may spin the facts, he and his false "*eclectic method*" accepted two false Gnostic manuscripts and threw out 18 Uncials, about 600 cursive copies, every known uncial or cursive (except Vatican and Sinai), and every known lectionary in the East.

> In addition to this, Dean Burgon cites the early versions or translations that had Mark 16:9-20:
>
> | | | |
> |---|---|---|
> | 1. 100-199 A.D. | Peshito Syriac |
> | 2. 100-199 A.D. | Vetus Itala (Old Latin) |
> | 3. 200·299 A.D. | Curetonian Syriac |
> | 4. 200-299 A.D. | Thebaic (Sahidic) Egyptian |
> | 5. 300-399 A.D. | Memphitic (Coptic) Egyptian |
> | 6. 350 A.D. | Gothic of Ulphilas |
> | 7. 382 A.D. | Latin Vulgate |
> | 8. 400-499 A.D. | Philoxenian  Syriac |
> | 9. 300-699 A.D.(?) | Ethiopic |
> | 10. 500-599 A.D.(?) | Georgian |

Does it seem to you "*the reasoned eclectic method takes all the evidence into account*"? It doesn't appear so to me. Remember, the first 6 of these early versions or translations were translated before the Gnostic Vatican and Sinai (c. 360 A.D.) were even in existence. Where did these early versions get Mark 16:9-10 unless they were there in the originals?

Here's one more example of proving that "*the reasoned eclectic method takes all the evidence into account*." is a lie. Below are listed 19 early Church Fathers who have cited Mark 16:9-10 in one of its unique places. Notice that the first 10 of these Church Fathers lived before the Vatican and Sinai manuscripts were ever in existence. So much for the lie that "*the reasoned eclectic method takes all the evidence into account*."

> | | | |
> |---|---|---|
> | 1. 100 | A.D. Papias (Mark 16:18) |
> | 2. 151 | A.D. Justin Martyr (Mark 16:20) |
> | 3. 180 | A.D. Irenaeus (Mark 16:19) |

| | |
|---|---|
| 4. 200 | A.D. Hippolytus (Mark 16:17-18) |
| 5. 256 | A.D. Vincentius (Mark 16:17-18) |
| 6. 250 | A.D. Acta Pilati (Mark 16:15-18) |
| 7. 200's-300's | A.D. Apostolical Constitutions (Mark 16:16) |
| 8. 325 | A.D. Eusebius (Mark 16:9-20) |
| 9. 325 | A.D. Marinus (Mark 16:9-20) |
| 10. 337 | A.D. Aphraates The Persian (Mark 16:9-20) |
| 11. 374-397 | A.D. Ambrose (Mark 16:15-18, 20) |
| 12. 400 | A.D. Chrysostom (Mark 16:9, 19-20) |
| 13. 331-420 | A.D. Jerome (Mark 16:9, 14) |
| 14. 395-430 | A.D. Augustine (Mark 16:12, 15-16) |
| 15. 430 | A.D. Nestorius (Mark 16:20 |
| 16. 430 | A.D. Cyril of Alexandria (Mark 16:20) |
| 17. 425 | A.D. Victor of Antioch (Mark 16:9-20) |
| 18. 500 | A.D. Hesychius (Mark 16:19) |
| 19.500's | A.D. Synopsis Scripturae Sacrae (Mark 16:9-20) |

# KJB Preserves The Originals In English

**STATEMENT #216.** (p. 419) "*Interestingly, declaring the King James Version to be the perfectly preserved pure Word of God does not resolve the problem of uncertainty. Current editions of the King James Versions differ in hundreds of places . . .*"

**COMMENT #216.** I have no problem of "*uncertainty*" with the King James Bible. The Cambridge 1769 edition is a good standard to be used, as we do in our *Defined King James Bible*, rather than the various perversions of it printed by various U.S.A. publishers.

As for "*declaring the King James Version to be the perfectly preserved pure Word of God*," I do not believe this at all. It is a position held by Peter Ruckman and his followers. Price should have identified Ruckman with this statement, but he did not. In this way, he is implying that all of us who stand for the King James Bible and the Hebrew, Aramaic, and Greek Words underlying it believe this Ruckmanite position.

I believe that the "*perfectly preserved pure Words of God*" are the Preserved original Hebrew, Aramaic, and Greek Words which underlie the King James Bible, not the King James Bible itself which is only an accurate translation in English of those Words.

# Price's False View of the KJB

**STATEMENT #217.** (p. 419) *"So why do some fundamentalists continue to proclaim that the King James Version is the **perfectly preserved, pure** Word of God for this generation?"*

**COMMENT #217.** I stand strong for the King James Bible and say this about it. I believe it is the only accurate, faithful, and true translation of the verbal, plenary, Preserved original Hebrew, Aramaic, and Greek Words.

> I don't use the words *"pure"* in referring to the King James Bible, but in referring to the verbal, plenary, Preserved original Hebrew, Aramaic, and Greek Words. Those Words are *"pure"* because they are God's Words. Only God is totally *"pure."* Anything that man does, regardless of its merits, cannot be termed perfectly *"pure."*

The same is true of Price's words *"perfectly preserved"* when referring to the King James Bible. I don't use this of any translation, including the excellent and accurate King James Bible.

> I reserve this phrase exclusively for the verbal, plenary, Preserved original Hebrew, Aramaic, and Greek Words.

Peter Ruckman and his followers are the ones Price has in mind. If he were fair in his writing, he should have singled out Ruckman and his crowd instead of leveling this charge at people like myself who take a stand for the King James Bible, but take decided exception to his charges about the use of these two terms.

# Preservation Not In Translations

**STATEMENT #218.** (p. 420) Price wrote: *"He preserved His Word in hundreds of ancient Bibles, witnesses to the text of Scripture."*

**COMMENT #218.** Price has a false view of Bible *"Preservation."*

> If all Price has in his false view of *"Bible Preservation,"* is *"hundreds of ancient Bibles,"* it is most defective indeed. That is not *"Bible Preservation"* at all, but only an extremely weak and partial *"preservation."* Real and genuine *"Bible Preservation"* is not believed by Price.

It is the verbal, plenary Preservation of the original Hebrew, Aramaic, and Greek Words of the Bible. He does not believe this has been done. I believe

God has kept His promise of Preservation in the Hebrew, Aramaic, and Greek Words underlying the King James Bible.

# Why Not Be Dogmatic For Truth?

**STATEMENT #219.** (p. 420) "*It is time to stop dogmatism, and go back to the historical doctrine of the Biblical text--appealing to the Hebrew and Greek texts as final authority and cross examining the witnesses in places of uncertainty.*"

**COMMENT #219.** Why does Price believe "*It is time to stop dogmatism*"? I am going to continue my dogmatism on the Bible's truth and the Bible's Words. I'm going to continue to believe God has kept his promises to Preserve His Hebrew, Aramaic, and Greek Words despite the avalanche of many Fundamentalist leaders who say God never promised to Preserve those Words. I am going to continue my "dogmatism" in believing those Hebrew, Aramaic, and Greek Words that God has Preserved, are those underlying the King James Bible.

# Price's Ruckman Smear Again

**STATEMENT #220.** (p. 420) Price was speaking about the "*King James Only view.*" He wrote: "*I witnessed its birth. It was conceived through the work of Seventh Day Adventist, Benjamin G. Wilkinson (1930), and through the works of Jasper James Ray (1955) and Edward F. Hills (1956). But these seeds remained relatively dormant until cultivated by the works of Peter S. Ruckman (1970) and David Otis Fuller (1970).*"

**COMMENT #220.** Price is trying wrongly to tie in the names mentioned with the false views and false doctrines of "*Peter S. Ruckman.*" This is what some refer to as "*dirty pool.*" It is reprehensible journalism.

> It is factually untrue for Price to imply that the views and beliefs of Peter S. Ruckman are the same as those of Wilkinson, Ray, Hills, and Fuller.

If he wants to prove it, let him try to find any quotation from any of these four men that show that they believe in the "*double inspiration*" of the King James Bible. That is, I defy him to find any quotation where these four men have said, as Ruckman has said, that the King James Bible as a new revelation that corrects the original Hebrew, Aramaic, and Greek Words of the Bible. If Price cannot produce such (and he cannot), let him keep quiet and apologize profusely for this grave and serious untruth.

# The Defects Of Modern Versions

**STATEMENT #221.** (p. 421) *"Of course, it is perfectly appropriate for a person or church to choose to use the King James Version, or any other version as a matter of preference. What is not acceptable is making the use of a translation an article of fundamental doctrine and a test of Fundamentalism and fellowship. It is time for the war against modern conservative translations to cease; they are not enemies of the Kingdom of God or tools of Satan."*

**COMMENT #221.** I totally disagree when Price pontificates: *"It is time for the war against modern conservative translations to cease."* In the first place, there is not a genuine *"modern conservative translation"* in the bunch! In one way or another, either by false techniques of translation (like the NKJV with over 2,000 examples of addition, subtraction, or changes in other ways [See **BFT #1442 @ $10.00 + $5.00 S&H**]) or by the inclusion of the heresies of the Gnostic heathenism. In the second place, I, for one, do not intend to cease my *"war"* against such so-called bible versions (with a small *"b."*)

Though Price does not want to make translations of God's Bible *"a test of Fundamentalism and fellowship,"* I certainly do. God says in His Word some very clear commands and principles as to what saved people are to do "**touch not the unclean thing** (2 Corinthians 6:17b). Or **if a soul touch any unclean thing,** whether it be a carcase of an unclean beast, or a carcase of unclean cattle, or the carcase of unclean creeping things, and if it be hidden from him; **he also shall be unclean, and guilty** (Leviticus 5:2). Depart ye, depart ye, go ye out from thence, touch no unclean thing; go ye out of the midst of her; **be ye clean, that bear the vessels of the LORD** (Isaiah 52:11).

I challenge Price and all of his anti-Textus Receptus and anti-King James Bible friends to buy these two books, read the pages mentioned that catalog either 158 or 356 Gnostic heresies contained in the Critical Text modern versions and then ask the Lord to (1) give them understanding of the serious doctrinal errors listed in these books, and (2) give them the wisdom, determination, and courage to lay them aside in favor of the Traditional Received Greek text and the King James Bible that accurately translates it.

The two books, as I have mentioned before are:

1. *Defending the King James Bible* (BFT #1594 @ $12.00 + $5.00 S&H), Chapter V

> 2. *Early Manuscripts, Church Fathers, and the Authorized Version* (BFT #3230 @ $20.00 + $5.00 S&H) on pages119-312.

# Modern Versions Have False Doctrine

**STATEMENT #222.** (p. 421) Price is talking about the so-called "*modern conservative translations*." He wrote: "*They declare neither false doctrine nor heresy*."

      **COMMENT #222.** Let's look at a few, of what I believe are, "*false doctrines or heresies*" as found in three of the "*modern conservative translations*." I believe that Price would agree that, for him, these three "*modern translations*" are "*conservative*." He falsely believes that there are no "*false doctrines or heresies*," in the NIV, the NASV, or the ESV. Here are just a few of what I consider to be.

+1. In 1 Timothy 3:16, the NIV, NASV, and ESV have "*false doctrine and heresy*" by omitting that the Lord Jesus Christ was "*God manifest in the flesh*."

+2. In Matthew 1:25, the NIV, NASV, and ESV have "*false doctrine and heresy*" by omitting that the Lord Jesus Christ was Mary's "*firstborn*" Son.

+3. In Matthew 18:11, the NIV, NASV, and ESV have "*false doctrine and heresy*" by omitting "*The son of man is come to save that which was lost*."

+4. In Luke 9:56, the NIV, NASV, and ESV have "*false doctrine and heresy*" by omitting "*For the Son of man is not come to destroy men's lives, but to save them*."

+5. In Luke 2:22, the NIV, NASV, and ESV have "*false doctrine and heresy*" by changing "*her*" purification to "*their*" purification thus thinking the Lord Jesus Christ needed "*purification*"and was therefore a sinner and needed to be purified.

+6. In Ephesians 3:9, the NIV, NASV, and ESV have "*false doctrine and heresy*"by omitting "*by Jesus Christ*," thus denying that the Lord Jesus Christ shared in the creation of the world with God the Father and God the Holy Spirit.

+7. In John 8:59, the NIV, NASV, and ESV have "*false doctrine and heresy*" by omitting "*going through the midst of them, and so passed by*" thus denying the omnipotence of the Lord Jesus Christ.

+8. In 2 Corinthians 4:14, the NIV, NASV, and ESV have "*false doctrine and heresy*" by changing "*by*" Jesus to "*with*" Jesus, thus denying that the Lord Jesus Christ has the power to raise the dead.

+9. In 1 Corinthians 5:7, the NIV, NASV, and ESV have "*false *doctrine and heresy*" by omitting "*for us*" thus denying the purpose of the sacrifice of the Lord Jesus Christ as substitutionary and vicarious.

✦10. Hebrews 1:3, the NIV, NASV, and ESV have "*false doctrine and heresy*" by omitting "*by Himself*," thus denying that the Lord Jesus Christ and He alone "*purged our sins*," not by any church, any priest, any saint, any ordinance, by Mary, or by any other person or thing.

✦11. In John 3:15, the NIV, NASV, and ESV have "*false doctrine and heresy*" by omitting "*should not perish*" thus denying the fact of the everlasting hell, which is the lake of literal fire, that awaits those who have not been saved by the Lord Jesus Christ,

✦12. In 2 Peter 2:17, the NIV, NASV, and ESV have "*false doctrine and heresy*" by omitting "*for ever*" thus denying the everlasting and eternal duration of hell, which is the lake of literal fire.

✦13. In John 6:47, the NIV, NASV, and ESV have "*false doctrine and heresy*" by omitting "*on me*" thus denying that the only Object of faith is the Lord Jesus Christ rather than making salvation dependent only on "*believing*."

✦14. In Romans 1:16, the NIV, NASV, and ESV have "*false doctrine and heresy*" by omitting "*of Christ*," thus failing to identify the specific and only thing that is "*the power of God unto salvation to every one that believeth*."

✦15. In Philippians 4:13, the NIV, NASV, and ESV have "*false doctrine and heresy*" by omitting "*Christ*" Who is the only One Who can "*strengthen*" those who are saved and can enable them to do "*all things*."

> Though Price might not consider these samples (and there are literally hundreds more) as having "*false doctrine and heresy*," I certainly do. I think many (if not all) of my readers will agree with me as well. Shame on Price for praising these "*modern conservative translations*" as haveing nothing to be concerned about doctrinally.

# Defined King James Bible Needed

**STATEMENT #223** (p. 421) "*Why should a preacher have to waste time explaining archaic words, phrases, and idioms, when he could better use the time declaring sound doctrine.*"

**COMMENT #223.** As far as "*explaining archaic words*," this is why our **Bible For Today** ministry has produced the *Defined King James Bible*. In this Bible, "*archaic words, phrases, and idioms*" are defined accurately in the footnotes. This enables people to continue to use the accurately translated King James Bible is superior to these other modern versions that are laden with false doctrines and Gnostic errors.

> The King James Bible which is superior in four areas: superior texts, superior translators, superior in translation technique, and superior theology.

The modern versions, though praised by Price, are defective and inferior in their texts, their translators, their technique of translation, and their theology. We should stay with the accurate and faithfully translated King James Bible.

> If Price has so much against the King James Bible why does he use it? To my mind, this is hypocrisy at the highest level.

# Prophets & Apostles Not "Inspired"

**STATEMENT #224.** Page 421, "*The words the Holy Spirit inspired the ancient prophets and apostles to write constitute the divinely inspired, infallible, inerrant Word of God.*"

**COMMENT #224.** Price once again demonstrates clearly that he doesn't have the faintest idea of what "*Biblical inspiration*" is. Proof of this is when he wrote: "*the Holy Spirit inspired the ancient prophets and apostles to write.* This is a heresy.

> The Holy Spirit did not "*inspire prophets*," He "*moved*" them (2 Peter 1:21). The Holy Spirit did not "*inspire apostles*," He "*moved*" them. On the contrary, God breathed-out or "*inspired Words*," not people (2 Timothy 3:16).

Price knows what this verse means: "*All scripture is given by inspiration of God . . .*" "*Scripture*" refers to the GRAPHE which are the "*Words*."

# The KJB Not Based On Stephanus

xxx **STATEMENT #225.** (p. 539) Price entitled his Appendix G, "*The Greek Text of the Authorized Version.*" He wrote: "*According to Bruce Metzger, a well known authority on the text of the New Testament, 'Stephanus' third edition [1550] became for many persons, especially in England, the received or standard text of the Greek New Testament.' This was the 'standard' text used by the translators of the Authorized Version. In addition, the translators had at their disposal the editions of Erasmus (1516, 1519, etc.), Beza (1589) and the Complutensian Polyglott (1514-1522).*"

**COMMENT #225.** It is totally false to say that

"*'Stephanus' third edition [1550]*" was *the 'standard' text used by the translators of the Authorized Version.*" Though on occasion this was used, the "*standard text*" underlying the King James Bible was Beza's 5th edition, 1598 (not 1589).    This is verified by the Preface of Dr. Frederick *Scrivener's Annotated Greek New Testament* [BFT #1670 @ $35.00 + $5.00 S&H].

# Index of Words and Phrases

# About the Author

The author of this book, Dr. D. A. Waite, received a B.A. (Bachelor of Arts) in classical Greek and Latin from the University of Michigan in 1948, a Th.M. (Master of Theology), with high honors, in New Testament Greek Literature and Exegesis from Dallas Theological Seminary in 1952, an M.A. (Master of Arts) in Speech from Southern Methodist University in 1953, a Th.D. (Doctor of Theology), with honors, in Bible Exposition from Dallas Theological Seminary in 1955, and a Ph.D. in Speech from Purdue University in 1961. He holds both New Jersey and Pennsylvania teacher certificates in Greek and Language Arts.

He has been a teacher in the areas of Greek, Hebrew, Bible, Speech, and English for over thirty-five years in ten schools, including one junior high, one senior high, four Bible institutes, two colleges, two universities, and one seminary. He served his country as a Navy Chaplain for five years on active duty; pastored three churches; was Chairman and Director of the Radio and Audio-Film Commission of the American Council of Christian Churches; since 1969, has been Founder, President, and Director of THE BIBLE FOR TODAY; since 1978, has been President of the DEAN BURGON SOCIETY; has produced over 700 other studies, books, audio cassettes, CD's, VCR's, or DVD's on various topics; and is heard on a thirty-minute weekly program, IN DEFENSE OF TRADITIONAL BIBLE TEXTS, on radio, and streaming on the Internet at BibleForToday.org, 24/7/365.

Dr. and Mrs. Waite have been married since 1948; they have four sons, one daughter, and, at present, eight grandchildren, and eight great-grandchildren. Since October 4, 1998, he has been the Pastor of the Bible For Today Baptist Church in Collingswood, New Jersey.

# Order Blank (p. 1)

Name:_____

Address:_____

City & State:_____Zip:_____

*Credit Card #:_____Expires:_____*

## Latest Books

[ ] Send *A Critical Answer to James Price's King James Only-ism* By Pastor D. A. Waite, 184pp, perfect bound ($11+$4 S&H)

[ ] Send *The KJB's Superior Hebrew & Greek Words* by Pastor D. A. Waite, 104 pp., perfect bound ($10+$4 S&H)

[ ] Send *Soulwinning's Versions-Perversions* by Pastor D. A. Waite, booklet, 28 pp. ($6+$3 S&H) fully indexed

[ ] Send *2 Timothy--Preaching Verse by Verse*, by Pastor D. A. Waite, 250 pages, perfect bound ($11+$5 S&H) fully indexed.

[ ] Send *A Critical Answer to God's Word Preserved* by Pastor D. A. Waite, 192 pp. perfect bound ($11.00+$4.00 S&H)

## The Most Recently Published Books

[ ] Send *8,000 Differences Between Textus Receptus & Critical Text* by Dr. J. A. Moorman, 544 pp., hrd. back ($20+$5 S&H)

[ ] *Early Manuscripts, Church Fathers, & the Authorized Version* by Dr. Jack Moorman, $20+$5 S&H. Hardback

[ ] Send *The LIE That Changed the Modern World* by Dr. H. D. Williams ($16+$5 S&H) Hardback book

[ ] Send *With Tears in My Heart* by Gertrude G. Sanborn. Hardback 414 pp. ($25+$5 S&H) 400 Christian Poems

## Preaching Verse by Verse Books

[ ] Send *2 Timothy--Preaching Verse by Verse*, by Pastor D. A. Waite, 250 pages, hardback ($11+$5 S&H) fully indexed.

[ ] Send 1 Timothy--Preaching Verse by Verse, by Pastor D. A. Waite, 288 pages, hardback ($14+$5 S&H) fully indexed.

[ ] Send *Romans--Preaching Verse by Verse* by Pastor D. A. Waite 736 pp. Hardback ($25+$5 S&H) fully indexed

Send or Call Orders to:

**THE BIBLE FOR TODAY**

**900 Park Ave., Collingswood, NJ 08108**

Phone: 856-854-4452; FAX:--2464; Orders: 1-800 JOHN 10:9

E-Mail Orders: BFT@BibleForToday.org; Credit Cards OK

# Order Blank (p. 2)

Name:_____

Address:_____

City & State:_____Zip:_____

Credit Card #:_____Expires:_____

## More Preaching Verse by Verse Books

[ ] Send *Colossians & Philemon--Preaching Verse by Verse* by
   Pastor D. A. Waite ($12+$5 S&H) hardback, 240 pages
[ ] Send *Philippians--Preaching Verse by Verse* by Pastor D.
   A. Waite ($10+$5 S&H) hardback, 176 pages
[ ] Send *Ephesians--Preaching Verse by Verse* by Pastor D. A.
   Waite ($12+$5  S&H) hardback, 224 pages
[ ] Send *Galatians--Preaching Verse By Verse* by Pastor D. A.
   Waite ($13+$5 S&H) hardback, 216 pages
[ ] Send *First Peter--Preaching Verse By Verse* by Pastor D.
   A.  Waite  ($10+$5 S&H) hardback, 176 pages

## Books on Bible Texts & Translations

[ ] Send *Defending the King James Bible* by DAW ($12+$5
   S&H) A hardback book, indexed with study questions
[ ] Send *BJU's Errors on Bible Preservation* by Dr. D. A.
   Waite, 110 pages, paperback ($8+$4 S&H) fully indexed
[ ] Send *Fundamentalist Deception on Bible Preservation* by
   Dr.Waite, ($8+$4 S&H), paperback, fully indexed
[ ] Send *Fundamentalist MIS-INFORMATION on Bible Ver-
   sions* by Dr. Waite ($7+$4 S&H) perfect bound, 136 pages
[ ] Send *Fundamentalist Distortions on Bible Versions* by
  Dr.Waite ($7  3 S&H) A perfect bound book, 80 pages
[ ] Send *Fuzzy Facts From Fundamentalists* by Dr. D. A.
   Waite ($8.00 + $4.00) printed booklet

Send or Call Orders to:
THE BIBLE FOR TODAY
900 Park Ave., Collingswood, NJ 08108
Phone: 856-854-4452; FAX:--2464; Orders: 1-800 JOHN 10:9
E-Mail Orders: BFT@BibleForToday.org;  Credit Cards OK

# Order Blank (p. 3)

Name:_____

Address:_____

City & State:_____Zip:_____

Credit Card #:_____Expires:_____

## More Books on Bible Texts & Translations

[ ] Send *Foes of the King James Bible Refuted* by DAW ($9
+$4 S&H) A perfect bound book, 164 pages in length

[ ] Send *Central Seminary Refuted on Bible Versions* by Dr.
Waite ($10+$4 S&H) A perfect bound book, 184 pages

[ ] Send *The Case for the King James Bible* by DAW ($7
+$3 S&H) A perfect bound book, 112 pages in length

[ ] Send *Theological Heresies of Westcott and Hort* by Dr. D.
A. Waite, ($7+$3 S&H) A printed booklet

[ ] Send *Westcott's Denial of Resurrection*, Dr. Waite ($4+$3)

[ ] Send *Four Reasons for Defending KJB* by DAW ($3+$3)

## More Books on Texts & Translations

[ ] Send *Holes in the Holman Christian Standard Bible* by Dr.
Waite ($4+$2 S&H) A printed booklet, 40 pages

[ ] Send *Contemporary Eng. Version Exposed*, DAW ($4+$2)

[ ] Send *NIV Inclusive Language Exposed* by DAW ($7+$3)

[ ] Send *24 Hours of KJB Seminar* (4 DVD's)by DAW($50.00)

## Books By Dr. Jack Moorman

[ ] Send Manuscript Digest of the N.T. (721 pp.) By Dr. Jack
Moorman, copy-machine bound ($50+$7 S&H)

[ ] *Early Manuscripts, Church Fathers, & the Authorized
Version* by Dr. Jack Moorman, $20+$5 S&H. Hardback

[ ] Send *Forever Settled--Bible Doc*uments *& History Survey*
by Dr. Jack Moorman, $20+$5 S&H. Hardback book

[ ] Send *When the KJB Departs from the So-Called "Majority
Text"* by Dr. Jack Moorman, $16+$5 S&H

Send or Call Orders to:
THE BIBLE FOR TODAY
900 Park Ave., Collingswood, NJ 08108
Phone: 856-854-4452; FAX:--2464; Orders: 1-800 JOHN 10:9
E-Mail Orders: BFT@BibleForToday.org; Credit Cards OK

# Order Blank (p. 4)

Name:_____

Address:_____

City & State:_____Zip:_____

Credit Card #:_____Expires:_____

## More Books By Dr. Jack Moorman

[ ] Send *Missing in Modern Bibles--Nestle/Aland/NIV Errors* by Dr. Jack Moorman, $8+$4 S&H

[ ] Send *The Doctrinal Heart of the Bible--Removed from Modern Versions* by Dr. Jack Moorman, VCR, $15 +$4 S&H

[ ] Send *Modern Bibles--The Dark Secret* by Dr. Jack Moorman, $5+$3 S&H

[ ] Send *Samuel P. Tregelles--The Man Who Made the Critical Text Acceptable to Bible Believers* by Dr. Moorman ($3+$1)

[ ] Send *8,000 Differences Between TR & CT* by Dr. Jack Moorman [$20 + $5.00 S&H] a hardback book

[ ] Send *356 Doctrinal Erors in the NIV & Other Modern Versions*, 100-large-pages, $10.00+$6 S&H

## Books By or About Dean Burgon

[ ] Send *The Revision Revised* by Dean Burgon ($25 + $5 S&H) A hardback book, 640 pages in length

[ ] Send *The Last 12 verses of Mark* by Dean Burgon ($15+$5 S&H) A hardback book 400 pages

[ ] Send *The Traditional Text* hardback by Burgon ($15+$5 S&H) A hardback book, 384 pages in length

[ ] Send *Causes of Corruption* by Burgon ($16+$5 S&H) A hardback book, 360 pages in length

Send or Call Orders to:
THE BIBLE FOR TODAY
900 Park Ave., Collingswood, NJ 08108
Phone: 856-854-4452; FAX:--2464; Orders: 1-800 JOHN 10:9
E-Mail Orders: BFT@BibleForToday.org;  Credit Cards OK

# Order Blank (p. 5)

Name:_____

Address:_____

City & State:_____Zip:_____

Credit Card #:_____Expires:_____

## More Books By or About Dean Burgon

[ ] Send *Inspiration and Interpretation*, Dean Burgon ($25+$5 S&H) A hardback book, 610 pages in length

[ ] Send *Burgon's Warnings on Revision* by DAW ($7+$4 S&H) A perfect bound book, 120 pages in length

[ ] Send *Westcott & Hort's Greek Text & Theory Refuted by Burgon's Revision Revised--Summarized* by Dr. D. A. Waite ($7.00+$4 S&H), 120 pages, perfect bound

[ ] Send *Dean Burgon's Confidence in KJB* by DAW ($3+$3)

[ ] Send *Vindicating Mark 16:9-20* by Dr. Waite ($3+$3S&H)

[ ] Send *Summary of Traditional Text* by Dr. Waite ($4 +$2)

[ ] Send *Summary of Causes of Corruption*, DAW ($4+$2)

[ ] Send *Summary of Inspiration* by Dr. Waite ($4+$2 S&H)

## More Books by Dr. D. A. Waite

[ ] Send *Making Marriage Melodious* by Pastor D. A. Waite ($7+$4 S&H), perfect bound, 112 pages

## Books by D. A. Waite, Jr.

[ ] Send *Readability of A.V. (KJB)* by D. A. Waite, Jr. ($6+$3)

[ ] Send *4,114 Definitions from the Defined King James Bible* by D. A. Waite, Jr. ($7.00+$4.00 S&H)

[ ] Send *The Doctored New Testament* by D. A. Waite, Jr. ($25+$5 S&H) Greek MSS differences shown, hardback

[ ] Send *Defined King James Bible* lg. prt. leather ($40+$10)

[ ] Send *Defined King James Bible* med. leather $35+$8.50)

Send or Call Orders to:
THE BIBLE FOR TODAY
900 Park Ave., Collingswood, NJ 08108
Phone: 856-854-4452; FAX:--2464; Orders: 1-800 JOHN 10:9
E-Mail Orders: BFT@BibleForToday.org; Credit Cards OK

# Order Blank (p. 6)

Name:_____

Address:_____

City & State:_____Zip:_____

Credit Card #:_____Expires:_____

### Miscellaneous Authors

[ ] Send *Wycliffe Controversies* by Dr. H. D. Williams,
     perfect bound, 311 pages @ $20.00 + $5.00 S&H
[ ] Send *The Pure Words of God* by Dr. H. D. Williams,
     perfect bound ($15.00 + $5 S&H)
[ ] Send *Hearing the Voice of God* by Dr. H. D. Williams,
      perfect bound ($18.00 + $5.00 S&H)
[ ] Send *The Attack on the Canon of Scripture* by Dr. H. D.
     Williams, perfect bound ($15.00 + $4.00 S&H)
[ ] Send *Word-For-Word Translating of The Received Texts* by
     Dr. H. D. Williams, 288 pages, paperback ($10+$5 S&H).
[ ] Send *Guide to Textual Criticism* by Edward Miller
     ($11+$4) a hardback book
[ ] Send *Scrivener's Greek New Testament Underlying the
     King James Bible*, hardback, ($14+$5 S&H)
[ ] Send *Scrivener's Annotated Greek New Testament*, by Dr.
     Frederick Scrivener:  Hardback--($35+$5 S&H);
     Genuine Leather--($45+$5 S&H)
[ ] Send *Why Not the King James Bible?--An Answer to James
     White's KJVO Book* by Dr.  K.  D.  DiVietro, $10+$5 S&H
[ ] Send Brochure #1: "Over *1000 Titles Defending the
KJB/TR"*  No Charge

Send or Call Orders to:
THE BIBLE FOR TODAY
900 Park Ave., Collingswood, NJ 08108
Phone: 856-854-4452; FAX:--2464; Orders: 1-800 JOHN 10:9
E-Mail Orders: BFT@BibleForToday.org;  Credit Cards OK

## Pastor D. A. Waite, Th.D., Ph.D.

# The Bible Battle

- **The Book Refuted.** This book is called a critical answer to *King James Onlyism: A New Sect*. The author is Dr. James D. Price who was formerly a Professor at Temple Baptist Seminary in Chattanooga, Tennessee, from 1972 to 2005.

- **The Positions Explained.** Price has taken a false position in two areas: (1) a disbelief in the preservation of the original Hebrew, Aramaic, and Greek Words, and (2) a strong opposition to those who maintain this position. He refers to them as "<u>King James Only</u>." This is a slanderous term implying those who believe the first area are Ruckmanites on the KJB.

- **The Purpose Revealed.** In this book, I have made COMMENTS on 225 of Price's STATEMENTS. I believe this is important because of the outlandish manner in which Price has repeatedly used clear inaccuracies and falsehoods in his book.

- **The Further Study.** The reader is encouraged to get three of my other recent books answering similar arguments on Bible versions and Bible preservation: (1) *Fundamentalist Deception on Bible Preservation* (**BFT #3234 @ $8.00 + $4.00 S&H**);. (2) *Bob Jones University's Errors on Bible Preservation* (**BFT #3259 @ $8.00 + $4.00 S&H**); and (3) *A Critical Answer to Michael Sproul's God's Word Preserved* (**BFT #3308 @ $11.00 + $4.00 S&H**). Learn to discern in this current battle for our Bible.

### www.BibleForToday.org

**BFT 3375 BK**          **ISBN #1-56848-063-6**

www.ingramcontent.com/pod-product-compliance
Lightning Source LLC
Chambersburg PA
CBHW051830090426
42736CB00011B/1740